MW00824766

Interactive Math Notebook: Geometry

Author: Schyrlet Cameron

Editor: Mary Dieterich

Proofreaders: Margaret Brown and April Albert

COPYRIGHT © 2019 Mark Twain Media, Inc.

ISBN 978-1-62223-765-4

Printing No. CD-405031

Mark Twain Media, Inc., Publishers
Distributed by Carson-Dellosa Publishing LLC

Visit us at www.carsondellosa.com

Table of Contents

Introduction

The *Interactive Math Notebook: Geometry* is designed to allow students to become active participants in their own learning. The book lays out an easy-to-follow plan for setting up, creating, and maintaining an interactive notebook.

An interactive notebook is simply a spiral notebook that students use to store and organize important information. It is a culmination of student work throughout the unit of study. Once completed, the notebook becomes the student's own personalized notebook and a great resource for reviewing and studying for tests.

The intent of the book is to help students make sense of new information. Textbooks often present more facts and data than students can process at one time. This book introduces each concept in an easy-to-read and easy-to-understand format that does not overwhelm the learner. The text presents only the most important information, making it easier for students to comprehend. Vocabulary words are printed in boldfaced type.

The book contains 28 lessons covering five units of study: Lines and Angles; Two-Dimensional Figures; Circles; Three-Dimensional Figures; and Perimeter, Area, and Volume. The units can be used in the order presented or in an order that best fits the classroom curriculum. Teachers can easily differentiate units to address the individual learning levels and needs of students. The lessons are designed to support state and national standards. Each lesson consists of two pages:

- **Input page:** essential information for understanding the lesson concepts and directions for creating the interactive page.
- **Output page:** hands-on activity such as a foldable or graphic organizer to help students process essential information from the lesson.

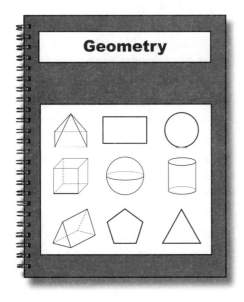

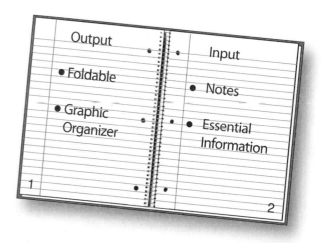

Organizing an Interactive Notebook

What Is an Interactive Notebook?

Does this sound familiar? "I can't find my homework…class notes…study guide." If so, the interactive notebook is a tool you can use to help manage this problem. An interactive notebook is simply a notebook that students use to record, store, and organize their work. The "interactive" aspect of the notebook comes from the fact that students are working with information in various ways as they fill in the notebook. Once completed, the notebook becomes the student's own personalized study guide and a great resource for reviewing information, reinforcing concepts, and studying for tests.

Materials Needed to Create an Interactive Notebook

- Notebook (spiral, composition, or binder with loose-leaf paper)
- Glue stick
- Scissors
- Colored pencils (we do not recommend using markers)
- Tabs

Creating an Interactive Notebook

A good time to introduce the interactive notebook is at the beginning of a new unit of study. Use the following steps to get started.

Step 1: *Notebook Cover*

Students design a cover to reflect the units of study. They should add their names and other important information as directed by the teacher.

Step 2: *Grading Rubric*

Take time to discuss the grading rubric with the students. It is important for each student to understand the expectations for creating the interactive notebook.

Step 3: *Table of Contents*

Students label the first several pages of the notebook "Table of Contents." When completing a new page, they add its title to the table of contents.

Step 4: *Creating Pages*

The notebook is developed using the dual-page format. The right-hand side is the input page where essential information and notes from readings, lectures, or videos are placed. The left-hand side is the output page reserved for foldable activities, charts, graphic organizers, etc. Students number the front and back of each page in the bottom outside corner (odd: LEFT-side; even: RIGHT-side).

Step 5: *Tab Units*

Add a tab to the edge of the first page of each unit to make it easy to flip to the unit.

Step 6: *Glossary*

Students reserve several pages at the back of the notebook where they can create a glossary of domain-specific terms encountered in each lesson.

Step 7: *Pocket*

Student need to attach a pocket to the inside of the back cover of the notebook for storage of handouts, returned quizzes, class syllabus, and other items that don't seem to belong on pages of the notebook. This can be an envelope, resealable plastic bag, or students can design their own pocket.

2

Left-hand and Right-hand Notebook Pages

Interactive notebooks are usually viewed open like a textbook. This allows the student to view the left-hand page and right-hand page at the same time. Teachers have several options for how to format the two pages. Traditionally, the right-hand page is used as the input or the content part of the lesson. The left-hand page is the student output part of the lesson. This is where the students have an opportunity to show what they have learned in a creative and colorful way. (Color helps the brain remember information better.) The notebook image on the right details different types of items and activities that could be included on each page.

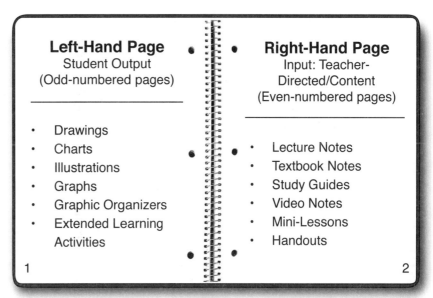

The format of the interactive notebook involves both the right-brain and left-brain hemispheres to help students process information. When creating the pages, start with the left-hand page. First, have students date the page. Students then move to the right-hand page and the teacher-directed part of the lesson. Finally, students use the information they have learned to complete the left-hand page. Below is an example of completed right- and left-hand pages.

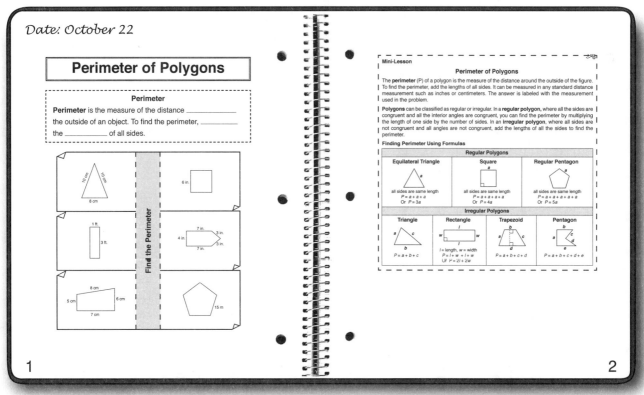

Left-Hand Page   **Right-Hand Page**

Interactive Notebook Grading Rubric

Directions: Review the grading rubric below. It lists the criteria that will be used to score your completed interactive notebook. Place this page in your notebook.

Interactive Math Notebook: Geometry Grading Rubric

Category	Excellent (4)	Good Work (3)	Needs Improvement (2)	Incomplete (1)
Table of Contents	Table of contents is complete.	Table of contents is mostly complete.	Table of contents is somewhat complete.	Attempt was made to include table of contents.
Organization	All pages in correct order. All are numbered, dated, and titled correctly.	Most pages in correct order. Most are numbered, dated, and titled correctly.	Some pages in correct order. Some are numbered, dated, and titled correctly.	Few pages in correct order. Few are numbered, dated, and titled correctly.
Content	All information complete, accurate, and placed in the correct order. All spelling correct.	Most information complete, accurate, and placed in the correct order. Most spelling correct.	Some information complete, accurate, and placed in the correct order. Some spelling errors.	Few pages correctly completed. Many spelling errors.
Appearance	All notebook pages are neat and colorful.	Most notebook pages are neat and colorful.	Some notebook pages are neat and colorful.	Few notebook pages are neat and colorful.

Student's Comments:

Teacher's Comments:

Student Instructions: Points, Lines, and Rays

Read the following information. Cut out the mini-lesson and attach it to the right-hand page of your interactive notebook. Use what you have learned to create the left-hand page.

Mini-Lesson

Points, Lines, and Rays

Geometry is a branch of mathematics that deals with points, lines, shapes, and space. Points, lines, segments, and rays are the basic terms of geometry used to describe and define other terms in geometry.

Common Terms

Term	Example	Symbol
Point: a single location or position (·) named with a capital letter	· *A*	·*A* *point A* *named by a capital letter*
Line: a straight line that is endless in both directions (↔)	*A*　*B*	$\overleftrightarrow{AB}$ or $\overleftrightarrow{BA}$ *line AB or line BA*
Line Ray: part of a line that extends in one direction from one endpoint (→)	*R*　*S*	$\overrightarrow{RS}$ *line ray RS*
Line Segment: part of a line between two endpoints (——)	*G*　*H*	$\overline{GH}$ *line segment GH*
Intersecting Lines: lines that meet at a point (∩)	*H*　*N* *M*　*O*　*K*	$\overleftrightarrow{NM} \cap \overleftrightarrow{KH}$ *line NM intersects line KH*
Parallel Lines: lines that never intersect (‖)	*A*　*B* *P*　*Q*	$\overleftrightarrow{AB} \parallel \overleftrightarrow{PQ}$ *line AB is parallel to line PQ*
Perpendicular Lines: lines that intersect to form right angles (⊥)	*U* *S*　*V*　*T*	$\overleftrightarrow{ST} \perp \overleftrightarrow{UV}$ *line ST is perpendicular to line UV*

Create Your Left-Hand Notebook Page

Step 1: Cut out the title and glue it to the top of the notebook page.

Step 2: Fill in the blank on the *What is Geometry?* flap book. Cut out the flap book. Cut on the solid lines to create four flaps. Apply glue to the back of the top section and attach it below the title. Under each flap, write the name of the symbol.

Step 3: Cut out the *Types of Lines* flap book. Apply glue to the back of the gray center section and attach it at the bottom of the page. Under each flap, write the name of the lines.

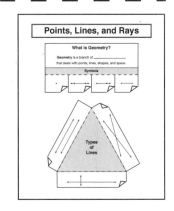

Points, Lines, and Rays

What is Geometry?

Geometry is a branch of _____

that deals with points, lines, shapes, and space.

Symbols

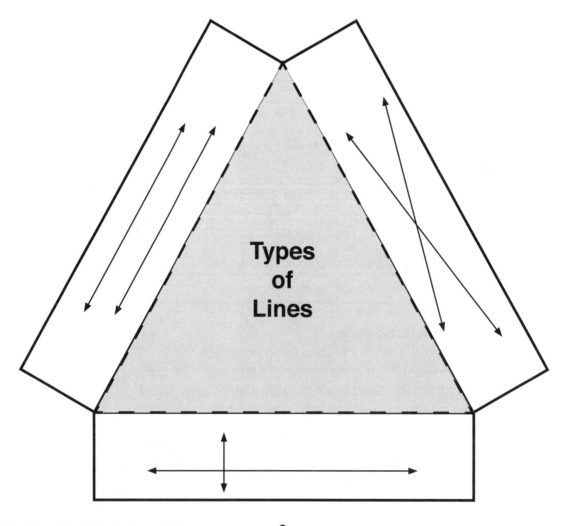

Types
of
Lines

Student Instructions: Identifying Angles

Read the following information. Cut out the mini-lesson and attach it to the right-hand page of your interactive notebook. Use what you have learned to create the left-hand page.

Mini-Lesson

Identifying Angles

An **angle** is formed by two rays, called the **sides**, sharing a common endpoint, called the **vertex**. The symbol used to represent an angle is ∠. A **protractor** is an instrument used to measure angles. Protractors measure angles in **degrees** (°). The inside of an angle is called the **interior**. The outside of an angle is called the **exterior**.

Parts of an Angle

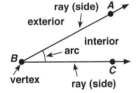

- Angles are often but not always marked using an **arc** or segment of a circle.

- The correct way to name an angle is either to write angle ABC, ∠ABC, ∠CBA, or ∠B. The middle letter of the three is always the vertex.

Types of Angles

acute angle	right angle	obtuse angle
an angle with a measure greater than 0° and less than 90°	an angle that measures 90°	an angle with a measure greater than 90° but less than 180°
straight angle	**reflex angle**	**full rotation angle**
an angle that measures 180°	an angle that is greater than 180° but less than 360°	an angle whose measure is exactly 360°

Create Your Left-hand Notebook Page

Step 1: Cut out the title and glue it to the top of the notebook page.

Step 2: Fill in the blanks on the *Parts of an Angle* piece. Cut out the four word pieces and glue them in the correct boxes on the diagram. Cut out the piece. Apply glue to the back and attach it below the title.

Step 3: Cut out the *Types of Angles* flap book. Cut on the solid lines to create six flaps. Apply glue to the back of the gray center section and attach it at the bottom of the page.

Step 4: Under each flap, draw the angle.

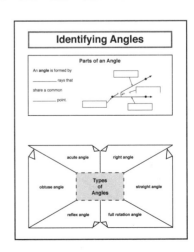

Identifying Angles

Parts of an Angle

An **angle** is formed by

_____ rays that

share a common

_____ point.

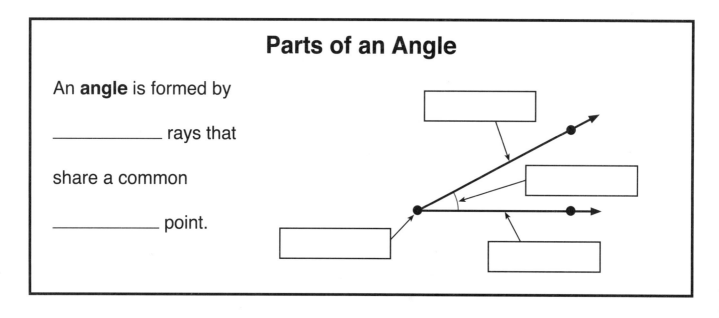

| arc | ray (side) | vertex | ray (side) |

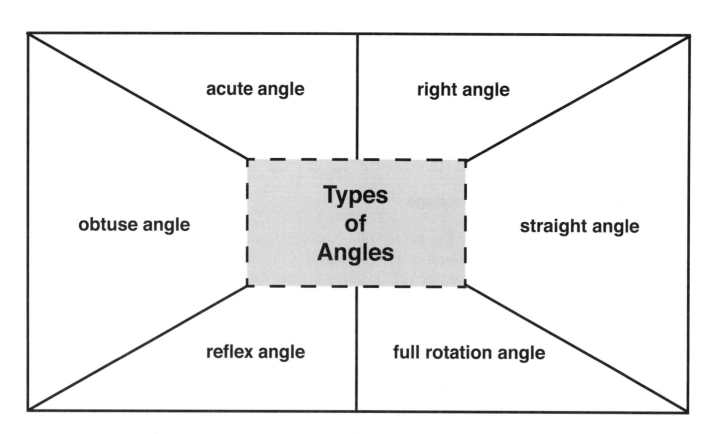

acute angle

right angle

Types of Angles

obtuse angle

straight angle

reflex angle

full rotation angle

Student Instructions: Measuring Angles

Read the following information. Cut out the mini-lesson and attach it to the right-hand page of your interactive notebook. Use what you have learned to create the left-hand page.

Mini-Lesson

Measuring Angles

Overview

An **angle** is formed by two lines, segments, or rays that share a common **endpoint** or **vertex**. A **protractor** is an instrument used to measure angles. Most protractors measure angles in **degrees** (°). One degree is written as 1°.

A protractor is marked in degrees with one scale that is read clockwise and another scale that is read counterclockwise.

Measuring Angles With a Protractor

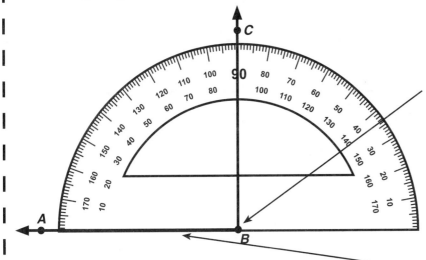

The center mark of the protractor is placed on the vertex of the angle. The endpoint that is shared by two rays that meet to form an angle is called a **vertex**.

To measure an angle, the base of the protractor is placed evenly on the line segment. One side of the angle must touch the zero mark.

The number of degrees in an angle is called its **measure** (m). To represent the measure of ∠ABC, we write m∠ABC = 90°.

Create Your Left-hand Notebook Page

Step 1: Cut out the title and glue it to the top of the notebook page.
Step 2: Fill in the blank on the *Protractor* flap book. Cut out the book. Cut on the solid lines to create four flaps. Apply glue to the gray center section. Attach the flap book below the title.
Step 3: Under each flap, write the meaning of the term.
Step 4: Cut out the *Measuring Angles* flap book. Cut on the solid lines to create three flaps. Apply glue to the back of the top section. Attach the flap book at the bottom of the page.
Step 5: Under each flap, write the measure of the angle.

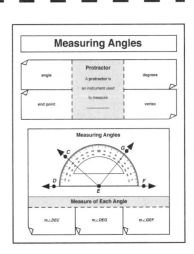

Measuring Angles

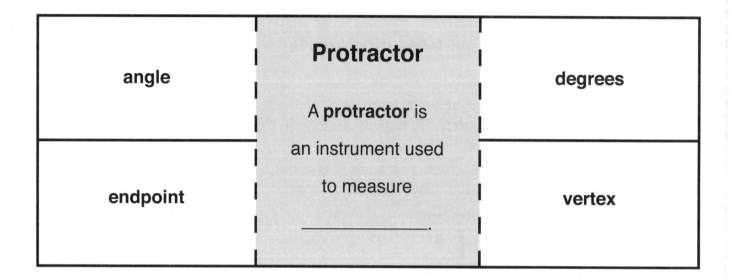

angle	**Protractor**	degrees
	A **protractor** is	
endpoint	an instrument used	vertex
	to measure	
	_____.	

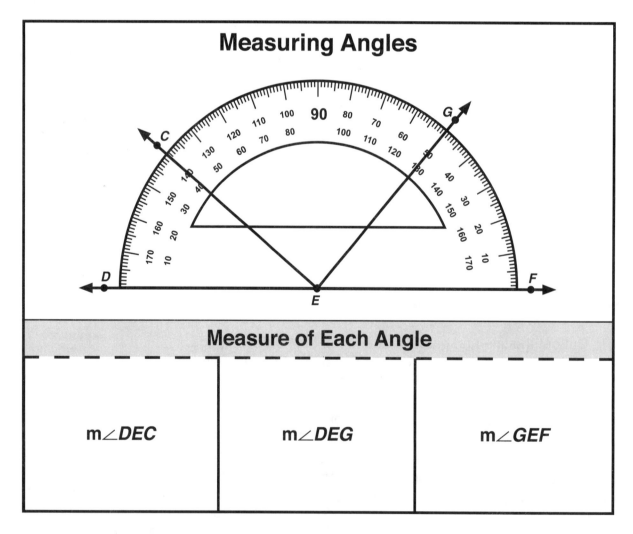

Measuring Angles

Measure of Each Angle

m∠DEC	m∠DEG	m∠GEF

Student Instructions: Polygons

Read the following information. Cut out the mini-lesson and attach it to the right-hand page of your interactive notebook. Use what you have learned to create the left-hand page.

Mini-Lesson

Polygons

A **two-dimensional** (2-D) figure is a shape that only has two dimensions (such as width and height). A **polygon** is a two-dimensional, closed figure that is formed by joining three or more line segments at their endpoints. Such shapes include squares, rectangles, triangles, and pentagons, but not circles or any shape that includes a curve.

Parts of a Polygon
The **sides** are the straight line segments that make up the polygon.

The **vertex** (plural: vertices) is a corner of the polygon. In any polygon, the number of sides and vertices (endpoints) are always equal.

Classifying Polygons

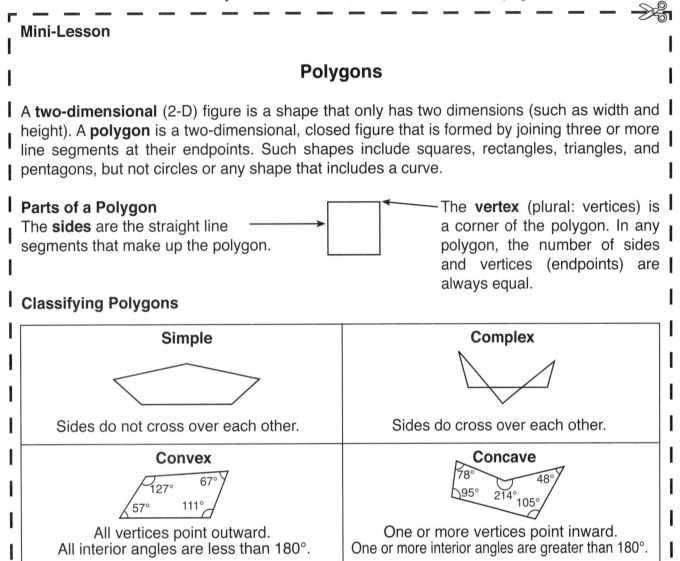

Simple	Complex
Sides do not cross over each other.	Sides do cross over each other.
Convex	**Concave**
All vertices point outward. All interior angles are less than 180°.	One or more vertices point inward. One or more interior angles are greater than 180°.

Create Your Left-hand Notebook Page

Step 1: Cut out the title and glue it to the top of the notebook page.

Step 2: Fill in the blanks on the *What is a Polygon?* definition piece. Cut out the piece. Apply glue to the back and attach it below the title.

Step 3: Cut out the *Classifying Polygons* flap book. Cut on the solid lines to create four flaps. Apply glue to the back of the gray center section and attach it at the bottom of the page.

Step 4: Under each flap, write the definition.

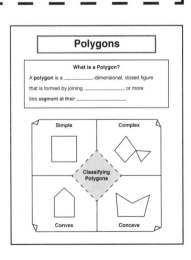

Polygons

What is a Polygon?

A **polygon** is a _____-dimensional, closed figure

that is formed by joining _____ or more

line segments at their _____.

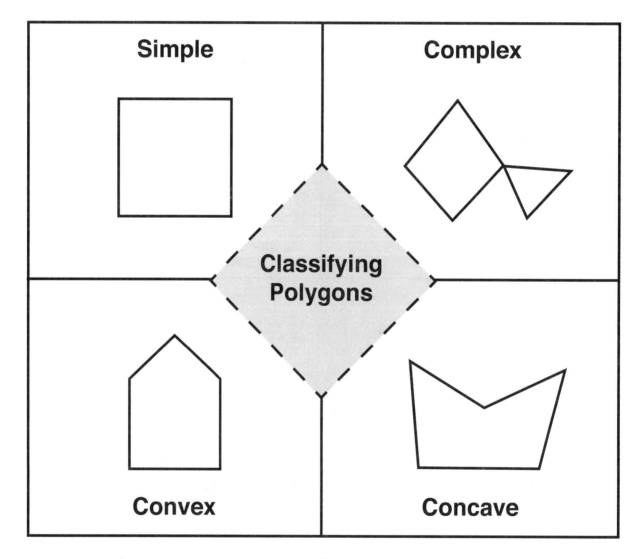

Student Instructions: Regular and Irregular Polygons

Read the following information. Cut out the mini-lesson and attach it to the right-hand page of your interactive notebook. Use what you have learned to create the left-hand page.

Mini-Lesson

Regular and Irregular Polygons

A **polygon** is a two-dimensional (2-D), closed figure that is formed by joining three or more line segments at their endpoints.

Regular and Irregular Polygons

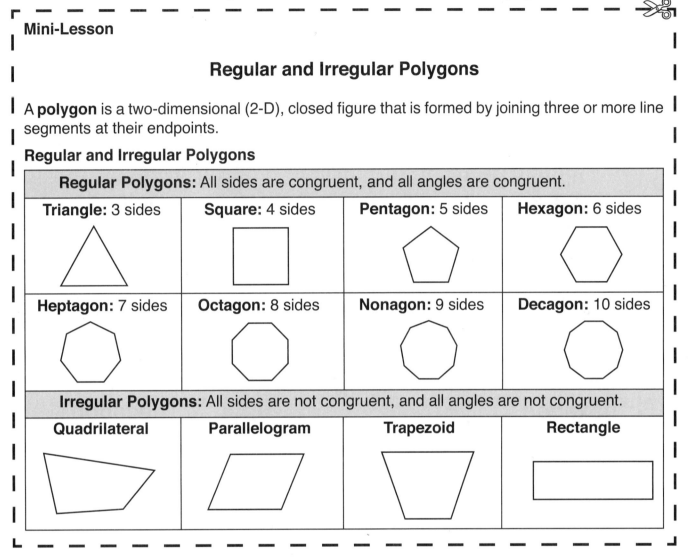

Regular Polygons: All sides are congruent, and all angles are congruent.			
Triangle: 3 sides	**Square:** 4 sides	**Pentagon:** 5 sides	**Hexagon:** 6 sides
Heptagon: 7 sides	**Octagon:** 8 sides	**Nonagon:** 9 sides	**Decagon:** 10 sides

Irregular Polygons: All sides are not congruent, and all angles are not congruent.			
Quadrilateral	**Parallelogram**	**Trapezoid**	**Rectangle**

Create Your Left-hand Notebook Page

Step 1: Cut out the title and glue it to the top of the notebook page.

Step 2: Fill in the blanks on the *Regular Polygons* flap book. Cut out the flap book. Cut on the solid lines to create eight flaps. Apply glue to the back of the gray center section and attach it below the title. Under each flap, write the number of sides for the polygon.

Step 3: Fill in the blanks on the *Irregular Polygons* flap book. Cut out the flap book. Cut on the solid lines to create four flaps. Apply glue to the back of the gray center section and attach it at the bottom of the page. Under each flap, write the name of the polygon.

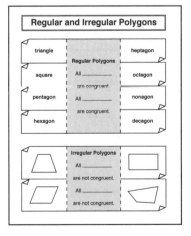

Regular and Irregular Polygons

triangle	**Regular Polygons**	heptagon
square	All _____	octagon
pentagon	are congruent.	nonagon
hexagon	All _____ are congruent.	decagon

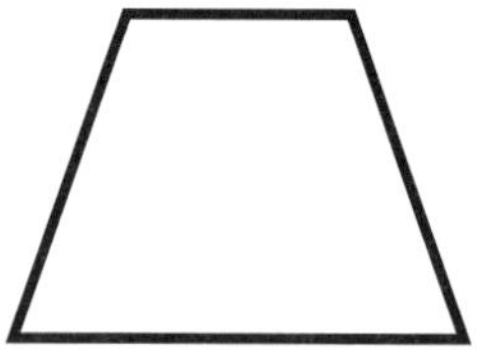

Irregular Polygons

All _____

are not congruent.

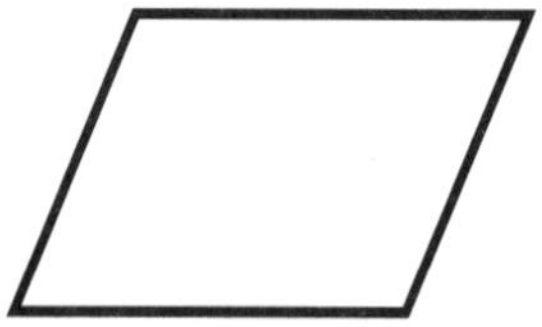

All _____

are not congruent.

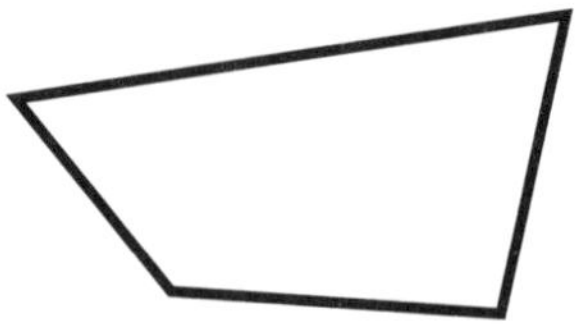

Student Instructions: Polygons Called Triangles

Read the following information. Cut out the mini-lesson and attach it to the right-hand page of your interactive notebook. Use what you have learned to create the left-hand page.

Mini-Lesson

Polygons Called Triangles

Triangles are polygons that have three interior angles formed by three sides. The symbol for angle is ∠. The sum of the three interior angles of a triangle is always 180°.

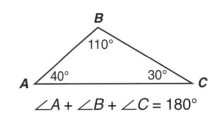

$\angle A + \angle B + \angle C = 180°$

Signs, Symbols, and Terms

Interior Angles	Points and Lines	Marking Angles
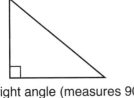 vertex — side — Interior Angles	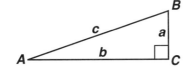	
Angles are formed by joining three line segments called sides at their endpoints or vertices.	Points at the vertex are labeled with capital letters such as *A, B,* and *C*. Straight lines are often labeled with lower-case letters, such as *a, b,* and *c*.	Angles are commonly marked using an arc (⌒) or segment of a circle.

Marking Right Angles	Congruent Angles	Congruent Sides
	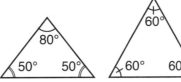	
A right angle (measures 90°) is marked with a square.	**Congruent angles** (same measure or angle size) are each marked with double arcs or tick marks (/).	**Congruent sides** (same length) are each marked with the same number of tick marks (/).

Create Your Left-hand Notebook Page

Step 1: Cut out the title and glue it to the top of the notebook page.

Step 2: Fill in the blanks on the *Triangles* flap book. Cut out the flap book. Cut on the solid lines to create four flaps. Apply glue to the back of the top section and attach it below the title. Under each flap, write the name of the symbol.

Step 3: Cut out the three *Question* flap pieces. Apply glue to the back of the gray tabs and attach them at the bottom of the page. Under each flap, write the answer.

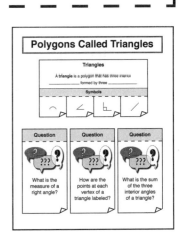

Polygons Called Triangles

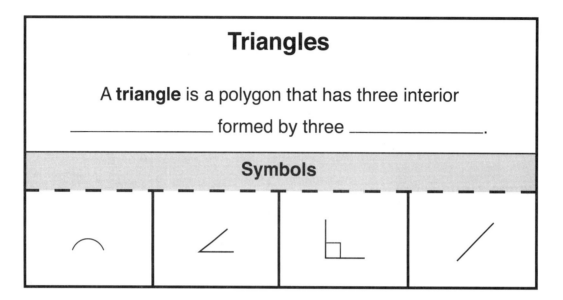

Triangles

A **triangle** is a polygon that has three interior

_____ formed by three _____.

Symbols

Question

What is the measure of a right angle?

Question

How are the points at each vertex of a triangle labeled?

Question

What is the sum of the three interior angles of a triangle?

Student Instructions: Classifying Triangles

Read the following information. Cut out the mini-lesson and attach it to the right-hand page of your interactive notebook. Use what you have learned to create the left-hand page.

Mini-Lesson

Classifying Triangles

Triangles are polygons that have three interior angles and three sides. Triangles are classified by the types of sides and angles they have. In some triangles, the length of the sides and/or size of the angles are **congruent**, or have the same measure. Example: An isosceles triangle has two sides with the same length (congruent) and two angles with the same size (congruent).

Classifying Triangles		
Right	**Acute**	**Obtuse**
one 90° angle two acute angles (angles less than 90°)	all angles are less than 90°	one angle measures more than 90°
Scalene	**Isosceles**	**Equilateral**
no congruent sides no congruent angles	two sides congruent two angles congruent	all sides congruent all angles congruent

Create Your Left-hand Notebook Page

Step 1: Cut out the title and glue it to the top of the notebook page.

Step 2: Fill in the blanks on the *Triangles* definition piece. Cut out the piece. Apply glue to the back and attach it below the title.

Step 3: Cut out the *Classifying Triangles* flap book. Cut on the solid lines to create six flaps. Apply glue to the back of the gray center section and attach it at the bottom of the page.

Step 4: Under each flap, write the name of the triangle.

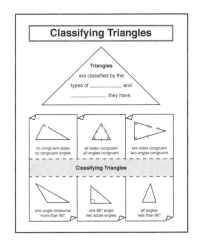

Classifying Triangles

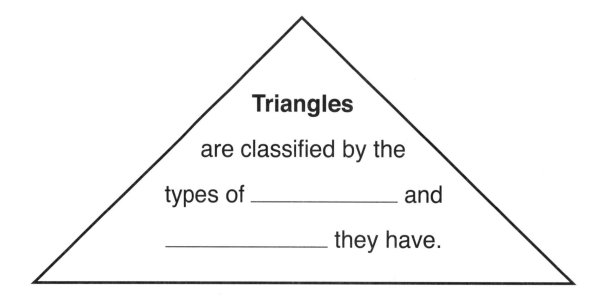

Triangles

are classified by the

types of _____ and

_____ they have.

no congruent sides
no congruent angles

all sides congruent
all angles congruent

two sides congruent
two angles congruent

Classifying Triangles

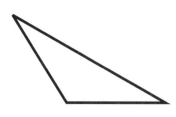

one angle measures
more than 90°

one 90° angle
two acute angles

all angles
less than 90°

Student Instructions: Polygons Called Quadrilaterals

Read the following information. Cut out the mini-lesson and attach it to the right-hand page of your interactive notebook. Use what you have learned to create the left-hand page.

Mini-Lesson

Polygons Called Quadrilaterals

A **quadrilateral** is a polygon with four **sides** and four **vertices** or corners. The total of the **interior angles** (angles inside the shape) in any quadrilateral is always 360°. Some quadrilaterals have **congruent angles** (same angle measure) and **congruent sides** (same length). Some quadrilaterals are also included in the definition of other types of polygons. For example, a square, rhombus, and rectangle are also classified as parallelograms. A square and rhombus also fit the definition of a rectangle.

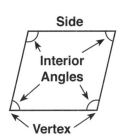

Classifying Quadrilaterals		
Square	**Rectangle**	**Parallelogram**
4 sides equal length 4 interior right angles opposite sides are parallel	4 interior right angles opposite sides are parallel and congruent	opposite sides are parallel and congruent
Trapezoid	**Rhombus**	**Kite**
one pair of parallel sides	all sides have equal length opposite sides are parallel opposite angles are congruent	two pairs of adjacent sides that are congruent

Create Your Left-hand Notebook Page

Step 1: Cut out the title and glue it to the top of the notebook page.

Step 2: Fill in the blanks on the *Quadrilaterals* flap book. Cut on the solid lines to create six flaps. Cut out the flap book. Apply glue to the back of the gray center section and attach it below the title.

Step 3: Under each flap, write the properties of each quadrilateral.

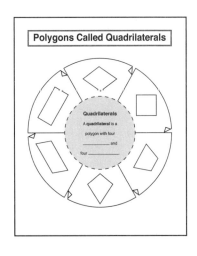

Polygons Called Quadrilaterals

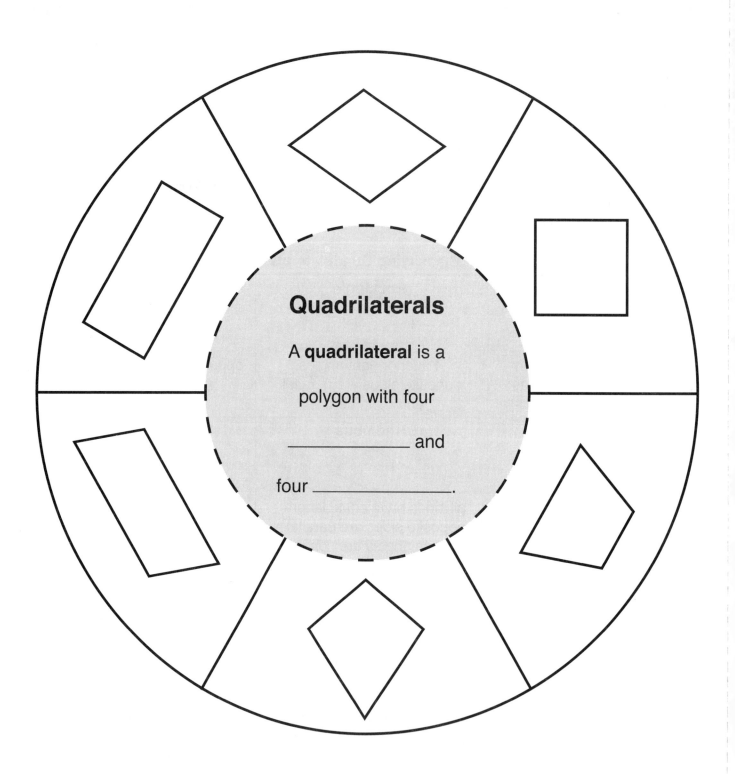

Quadrilaterals

A **quadrilateral** is a

polygon with four

_____ and

four _____.

Student Instructions: Congruent or Similar?

Read the following information. Cut out the mini-lesson and attach it to the right-hand page of your interactive notebook. Use what you have learned to create the left-hand page.

Mini-Lesson

Congruent or Similar?

The words *similar* and *congruent* are used to describe geometrical figures.

Similar figures have the same shape but can be different sizes. The corresponding interior angles are **congruent** (have the same measure) and the corresponding sides are proportional.

Congruent figures have the same size and the same shape. The corresponding sides have the same measure, and the corresponding angles have the same measure. Tick marks (/) and arcs (⌒) are often used to denote the corresponding parts of congruent figures. The symbol used to denote congruent is ≅.

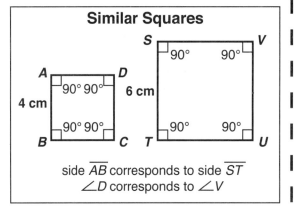

Similar Squares

side $\overline{AB}$ corresponds to side $\overline{ST}$
∠*D* corresponds to ∠*V*

Congruent Polygons

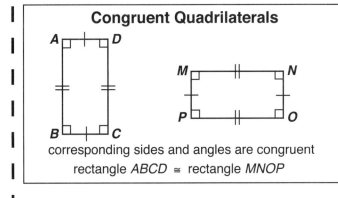

Congruent Quadrilaterals

corresponding sides and angles are congruent
rectangle *ABCD* ≅ rectangle *MNOP*

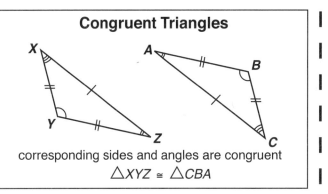

Congruent Triangles

corresponding sides and angles are congruent
△*XYZ* ≅ △*CBA*

Create Your Left-hand Notebook Page

Step 1: Cut out the title and glue it to the top of the notebook page.

Step 2: Cut out the *What is the Difference?* flap book. Apply glue to the back of the gray center section and attach it below the title. Under each flap, write the definition.

Step 3: Cut out the *Congruent or Similar?* flap book. Cut on the solid lines to create two flaps. Apply glue to the back of the gray section and attach it at the bottom of the page. Cut out the two picture pieces. Under each flap, glue the correct piece.

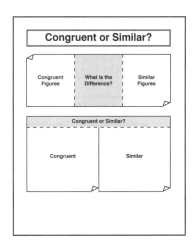

Congruent or Similar?

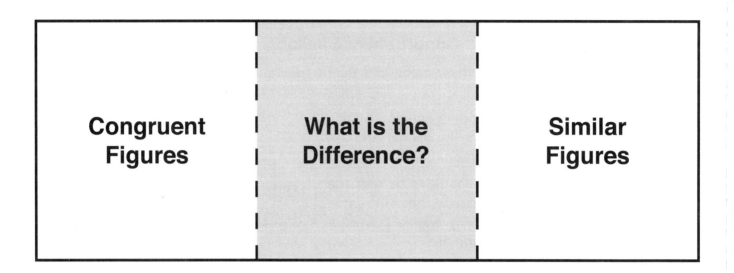

| Congruent Figures | What is the Difference? | Similar Figures |

Congruent or Similar?

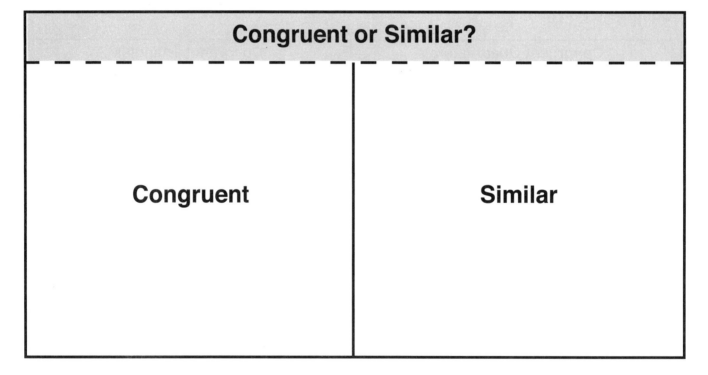

| Congruent | Similar |

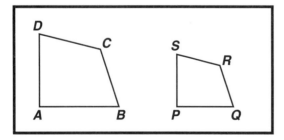

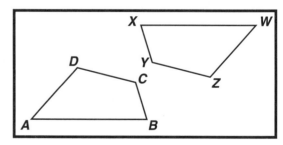

Student Instructions: Lines of Symmetry

Read the following information. Cut out the mini-lesson and attach it to the right-hand page of your interactive notebook. Use what you have learned to create the left-hand page.

Mini-Lesson

Lines of Symmetry

Symmetry occurs when two halves of a figure mirror each other across a line. The line that divides the figure into two mirror images is called the **line of symmetry**. The line of symmetry must separate the figure into two **congruent parts**, same size and shape. When the figure is folded over the line of symmetry, the two halves fit together. Some figures have more than one line of symmetry. The line of symmetry does not have to be vertical; it can go in any direction.

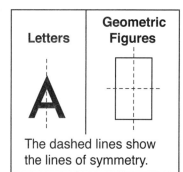

The dashed lines show the lines of symmetry.

Lines of Symmetry in Polygons

Regular Polygons: All sides are congruent (same length) and all angles are congruent (same measure). Number of sides = Number of lines of symmetry			
Equilateral Triangle: 3 sides 3 lines of symmetry	**Square:** 4 sides 4 lines of symmetry	**Pentagon:** 5 sides 5 lines of symmetry	**Hexagon:** 6 sides 6 lines of symmetry
Irregular Polygons: All sides are not congruent and all angles are not congruent.			
Rectangle	Parallelogram	Trapezoid	Rhombus
2 lines of symmetry	No line of symmetry	1 line of symmetry / No line of symmetry	2 lines of symmetry

Create Your Left-hand Notebook Page

Step 1: Cut out the title and glue it to the top of the notebook page.

Step 2: Fill in the blanks on the *Lines of Symmetry* pocket. Cut out the pocket. Fold back the gray tabs on the dotted lines. Apply glue to the tabs and attach the pocket below the title.

Step 3: Cut out the six shapes pieces. Fold each shape to find all lines of symmetry. Draw the lines on each shape. Write the total number of lines of symmetry on the back of each shape. Place each shape in the pocket.

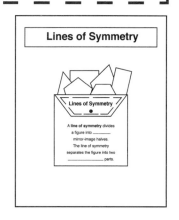

Lines of Symmetry

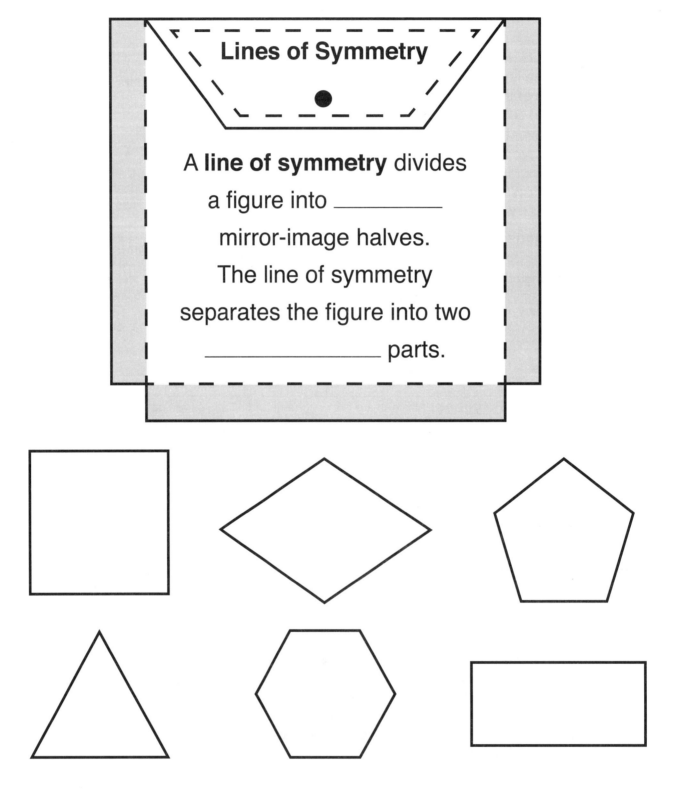

Lines of Symmetry

A **line of symmetry** divides a figure into _____ mirror-image halves. The line of symmetry separates the figure into two _____ parts.

Student Instructions: Parts of a Circle

Read the following information. Cut out the mini-lesson and attach it to the right-hand page of your interactive notebook. Use what you have learned to create the left-hand page.

Mini-Lesson

Parts of a Circle

A **circle** is a round, two-dimensional figure. All points on the edge of the circle are the same distance from the **center point**. A circle is named by its center. For example (see below), if point *B* is the center of the circle, then the name of the circle is circle *B*.

Parts of a Circle

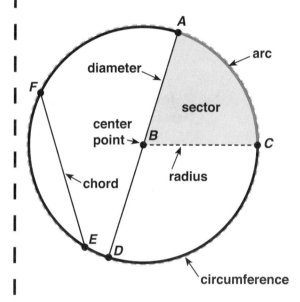

Circumference: the distance around the outer edge of a circle

Radius: the distance from the center of a circle to a point on the circle

Chord: a line segment that connects one point on the edge of a circle with another point on the circle (Some chords pass through the center and some do not.)

Diameter: the distance across a circle through its center point (The diameter is a chord that passes through the center point of a circle.); the diameter of a circle is twice as long as the radius

Sector: a pie-shaped portion of the area of a circle

Arc: a line that links two points on a circle or curve

Central angle: an angle that has its vertex at the center of a circle; $\angle ABC$ is the central angle of the circle shown at the left; there are 360° in a circle

Create Your Left-hand Notebook Page

Step 1: Cut out the title and glue it to the top of the notebook page.

Step 2: Fill in the blanks on the *Circle Diagram* piece. Cut out the word pieces and glue in the correct boxes on the diagram. Cut out the diagram piece. Apply glue to the back and attach it below the title on the left.

Step 3: Use a colored pencil to trace over or shade in the part of the circle named on the *Chord* and *Sector* flap pieces. Cut out the two flap pieces. Apply glue to the back of the gray tabs and attach them below the title on the right.

Step 4: Under each flap, write the definition.

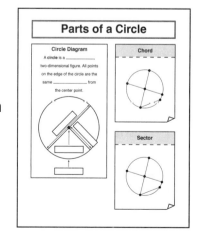

Parts of a Circle

Circle Diagram

A **circle** is a _____, two-dimensional figure. All points on the edge of the circle are the same _____ from the center point.

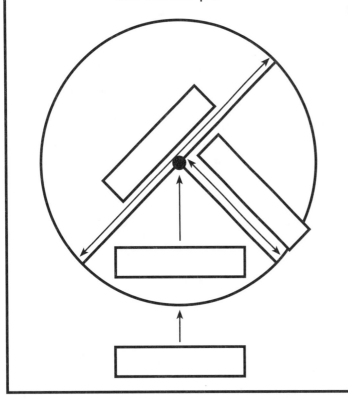

center point	radius
circumference	diameter

Chord

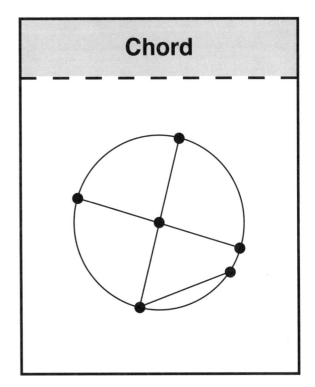

Sector

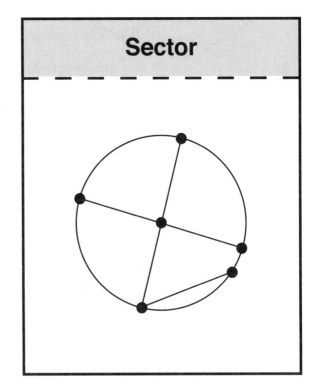

Student Instructions: Radius and Diameter

Read the following information. Cut out the mini-lesson and attach it to the right-hand page of your interactive notebook. Use what you have learned to create the left-hand page.

Mini-Lesson

The Radius and Diameter of a Circle

A **circle** is a round, two-dimensional figure. All points on the edge of the circle are the same distance from the **center point**.

Radius	Diameter
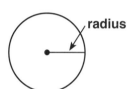	
Radius: the distance from the center point to the edge of the circle	**Diameter:** the distance across a circle through its center point; the diameter of a circle is twice as long as the radius

Finding Diameter	**Finding Radius**
When given the radius of a circle, it is possible to calculate the diameter of that circle by multiplying the radius by 2. The formula for finding the diameter of a circle is $d = 2r$ or $2 \times r$.	When given the diameter of a circle, it is possible to calculate the radius of that circle by dividing the diameter by 2. The formula for finding the radius of a circle is $r = \dfrac{d}{2}$

$$d = 2r$$
$$d = 2 \times 4 \text{ cm}$$
$$d = 8 \text{ cm}$$

$$r = \dfrac{d}{2}$$
$$r = 8 \text{ cm} \div 2$$
$$r = 4 \text{ cm}$$

Create Your Left-hand Notebook Page

Step 1: Cut out the title and glue it to the top of the notebook page.

Step 2: Fill in the blanks on the *Circles* piece. Cut out the piece. Apply glue to the back and attach it below the title.

Step 3: Cut out the *What is the Diameter?* and *What is the Radius?* flap pieces. Apply glue to the back of the gray tabs and attach them at the bottom of the page.

Step 4: Under each flap, write the formula and answer the question. Show your work.

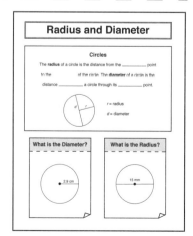

Radius and Diameter

Circles

The **radius** of a circle is the distance from the _____ point

to the _____ of the circle. The **diameter** of a circle is the

distance _____ a circle through its _____ point.

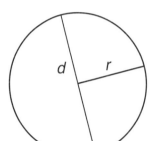

r = radius

d = diameter

What is the Diameter?

2.9 cm

What is the Radius?

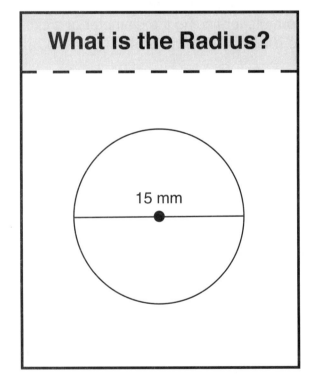

15 mm

Student Instructions: Circumference of a Circle

Read the following information. Cut out the mini-lesson and attach it to the right-hand page of your interactive notebook. Use what you have learned to create the left-hand page.

Mini-Lesson

Circumference of a Circle

In the circle to the right, **C** stands for **circumference**, the distance around the circle; **r** represents **radius**, a line segment that joins the center of the circle with any point on its circumference; and **d** means **diameter**, a straight line passing through the center of a circle, ending at the circumference.

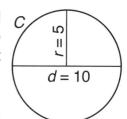

The circumference of a circle can be calculated using the formulas below. In the formula, the Greek letter **π** is called **pi**. The value of **pi** is approximately 3.14.

$$C = \pi d \text{ (pi x diameter) or } C = 2\pi r \text{ (2 x pi x radius)}$$

Find Circumference

Example: Diameter is 2 m $C = \pi d$ $C = 3.14 \times 2 \text{ m}$ $C = 6.28 \text{ m}$	Example: Radius is 4 cm Step #1: Find Diameter $d = 2r$ $d = 2 \times 4 \text{ cm}$ $d = 8 \text{ cm}$ Step #2: Find Circumference $C = \pi d$ $C = 3.14 \times 8 \text{ cm}$ $C = 25.12 \text{ cm}$

Create Your Left-hand Notebook Page

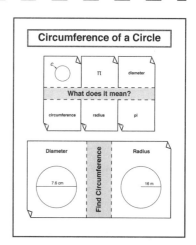

Step 1: Cut out the title and glue it to the top of the notebook page.

Step 2: Cut out the *What does it mean?* flap book. Cut on the solid lines to create six flaps. Apply glue to the back of the gray center section and attach it below the title.

Step 3: Under each flap, write the definition.

Step 4: Cut out the *Find Circumference* flap book. Apply glue to the back of the gray center section and attach it at the bottom of the page.

Step 5: Under each flap, write the formula and calculate the circumference. Show your work.

Circumference of a Circle

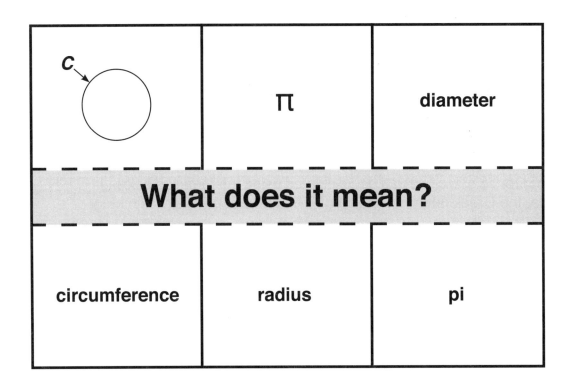

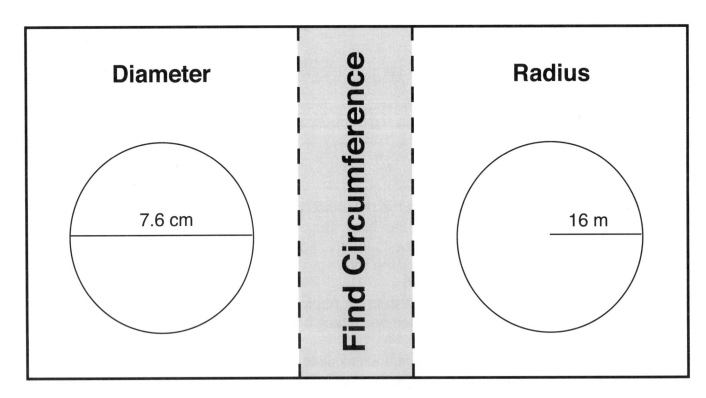

Student Instructions: Area of a Circle

Read the following information. Cut out the mini-lesson and attach it to the right-hand page of your interactive notebook. Use what you have learned to create the left-hand page.

Mini-Lesson

Area of a Circle

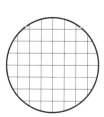

The **area** of a circle is the number of square units inside that circle. Area is measured in **square units** (sq. units) such as in², ft², cm², and m². The area of a circle is calculated by using the formulas below. The Greek letter π is called **pi**. The value of pi is approximately 3.14. To square a number means to multiply it by itself.

- **When you know radius:**
  Area equals π (pi) times the radius squared: $A = \pi r^2$ or $A = \pi \times r \times r$

- **When you know diameter:**
  Step 1:   Calculate the radius — radius equals diameter divided by 2: $\dfrac{d}{2}$

  Step 2:   Calculate area — Area equals π (pi) times the radius squared:
  $A = \pi r^2$ or $A = \pi \times r \times r$

Area of a Circle

Example 1: Radius is 3 m	Example 2: Diameter is 8 m
Formula:	Formulas:
$A = \pi \times r^2$	Step #1: Find Radius Step #2: Find Area
$A = \pi \times r \times r$	$r = \dfrac{d}{2}$ $A = \pi \times r^2$
$A = 3.14 \times 3\,m \times 3\,m$	$A = \pi \times r \times r$
$A = 3.14 \times 9$	$r = 8 \div 2$ $A = 3.14 \times 4\,m \times 4\,m$
$A = 28.26\ m^2$	$r = 4\,m$ $A = 3.14 \times 16$
	$A = 50.24\ m^2$

Create Your Left-hand Notebook Page

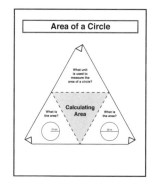

Step 1: Cut out the title and glue it to the top of the notebook page.
Step 2: Cut out the *Calculating Area* flap book. Apply glue to the back of the gray center section and attach it below the title.
Step 3: Under each flap, answer the question.

Area of a Circle

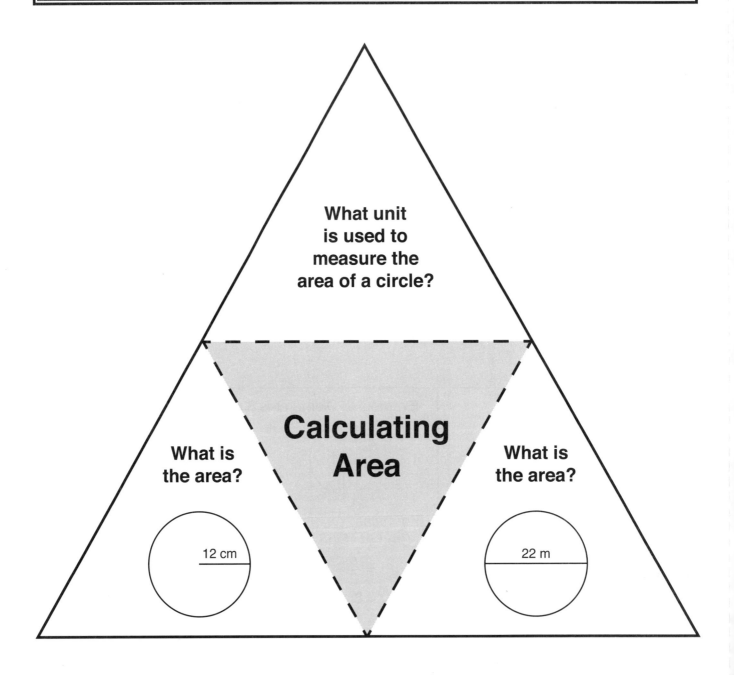

What unit
is used to
measure the
area of a circle?

What is
the area?

**Calculating
Area**

What is
the area?

12 cm

22 m

Student Instructions: Three-Dimensional Figures

Read the following information. Cut out the mini-lesson and attach it to the right-hand page of your interactive notebook. Use what you have learned to create the left-hand page.

Mini-Lesson

Three-Dimensional Figures

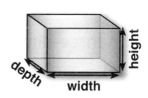

Solid geometry is the study of three-dimensional space.
It is called **three-dimensional (3-D)** because there are three dimensions: width, depth, and height. Three-dimensional figures take up space or volume.

Examples:

Properties of Three-Dimensional figures
- **volume:** the measure of the amount of space inside of a solid figure
- **surface area:** the total surface area of all the faces and bases of a figure

A **face** is the flat surface on a solid figure. Faces are in the form of plane shapes, such as triangles, rectangles, and squares.

An **edge** joins one vertex with another. The dashed lines represent edges that are on the back side of the figure.

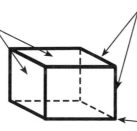

A **vertex** is a corner.

Types of Three-Dimensional Figures

Polyhedron (has all flat surfaces)	Non-Polyhedron (has surfaces that are not flat)

Create Your Left-hand Notebook Page

Step 1: Cut out the title and glue it to the top of the notebook page.

Step 2: Fill in the blank on the *3-D* definition piece. Cut out the piece. Apply glue to the back and attach it below the title.

Step 3: Cut out the *What's the Difference?* flap book. Cut on the solid lines to create two flaps. Apply glue to the back of the gray tab and attach it below the title. Under each flap, write the definition.

Step 4: Complete the chart. Cut out the chart. Apply glue to the back and attach it at the bottom of the page.

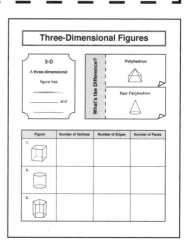

Three-Dimensional Figures

3-D

A **three-dimensional**

figure has

_____,

_____, and

_____.

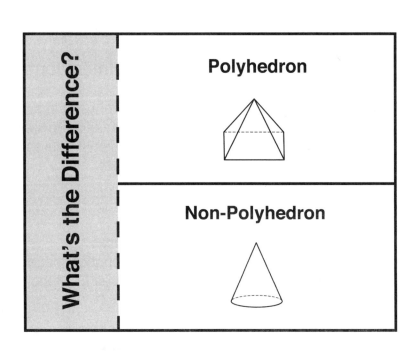

Figure	Number of Vertices	Number of Edges	Number of Faces
1. 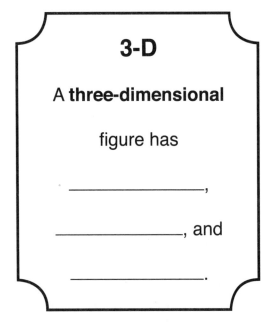			
2.			
3.			

Student Instructions: Prisms

Read the following information. Cut out the mini-lesson and attach it to the right-hand page of your interactive notebook. Use what you have learned to create the left-hand page.

Mini-Lesson

Prisms

A **prism** is a polyhedron with two parallel bases that are congruent polygons and faces that are parallelograms. A prism is named by the shape of its base.

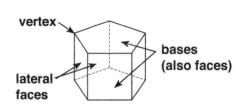

Faces, Edges, and Vertices

You can count the number of faces, edges, and vertices of a prism. A **face** is the flat surface on a solid figure. Faces of prisms are shapes such as triangles, rectangles, and squares. **Lateral faces** are the flat surfaces that are not bases. An **edge** joins one vertex with another. A **vertex** is a corner. The dashed lines represent edges that are on the back side of the figure.

Types of Prisms

Regular Prisms	Irregular Prisms	A Special Regular Prism

bases are regular polygons	bases are irregular polygons	**Cube** box-shaped 6 square faces all right angles

Classify Prisms by Their Bases

Triangular Prism	Rectangular Prism	Pentagonal Prism	Hexagonal Prism
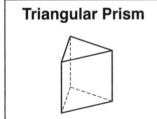			

Create Your Left-hand Notebook Page

Step 1: Cut out the title and glue it to the top of the notebook page.

Step 2: Fill in the blanks on the *Classifying Prisms* flap book. Apply glue to the back of the gray center section and attach it below the title.

Step 3: Under each flap, write the name of the prism.

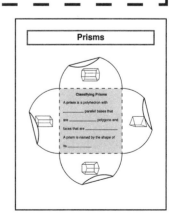

Prisms

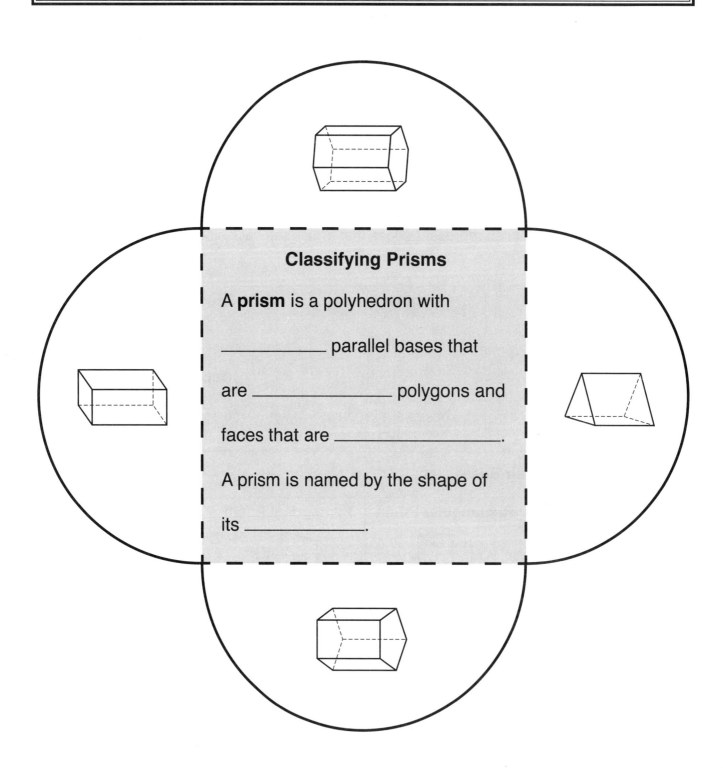

Classifying Prisms

A **prism** is a polyhedron with

_____ parallel bases that

are _____ polygons and

faces that are _____.

A prism is named by the shape of

its _____.

Student Instructions: Pyramids

Read the following information. Cut out the mini-lesson and attach it to the right-hand page of your interactive notebook. Use what you have learned to create the left-hand page.

Mini-Lesson

Pyramids

A **pyramid** is a polyhedron with triangles for lateral faces and one base. The **base** can be any polygon. A pyramid is classified by the shape of the base.

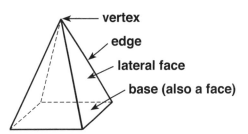

Faces, Edges, and Vertices

You can count the number of faces, edges, and vertices of a pyramid. A **face** is the flat surface on a solid figure. **Lateral faces** are the flat surfaces that are not bases. For a pyramid, the lateral faces are all triangles. An **edge** joins one vertex with another. A **vertex** is a corner. The dashed lines represent edges that are on the back side of the figure.

Classify Pyramids by Their Bases

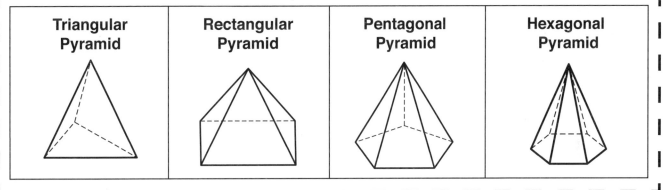

Triangular Pyramid	Rectangular Pyramid	Pentagonal Pyramid	Hexagonal Pyramid

Create Your Left-hand Notebook Page

Step 1: Cut out the title and glue it to the top of the notebook page.

Step 2: Fill in the blank on the *What is a Pyramid?* definition piece. Cut out the piece. Apply glue to the back and attach it below the title.

Step 3: Cut out the *Parts of a Pyramid* flap book. Cut on the solid lines to create four flaps. Apply glue to the back of the gray tab and attach it on the left side of the page. Under each flap, write the name of the part of the pyramid indicated by the arrow.

Step 4: Cut out the *Classifying Pyramids* flap book. Cut on the solid lines to create four flaps. Apply glue to the back of the gray tab and attach it to the right side of the page. Under each flap, write the name of the pyramid.

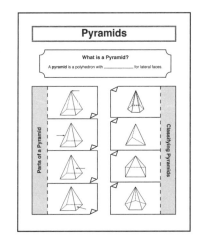

37

Pyramids

What is a Pyramid?

A **pyramid** is a polyhedron with _____ for lateral faces.

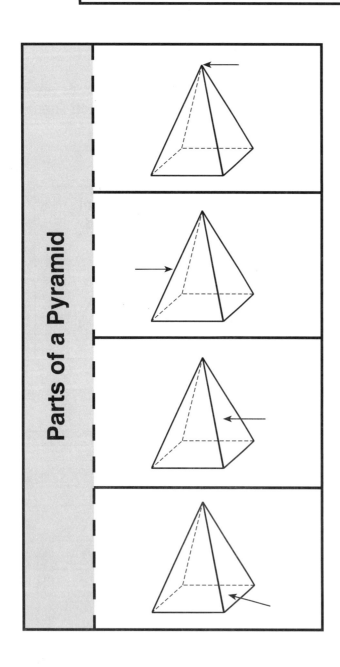

Parts of a Pyramid

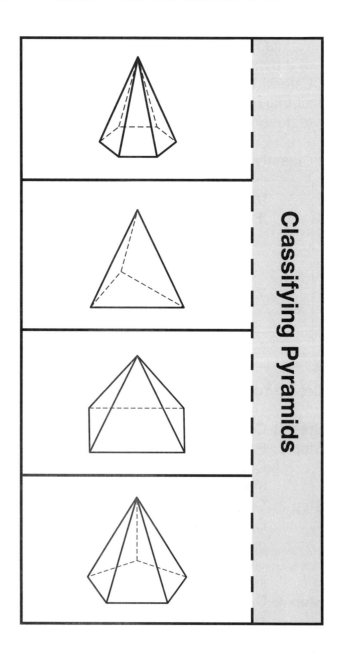

Classifying Pyramids

Student Instructions: Curved Solid Objects

Read the following information. Cut out the mini-lesson and attach it to the right-hand page of your interactive notebook. Use what you have learned to create the left-hand page.

Mini-Lesson

Curved Solid Objects

A **curved solid object** is a three-dimensional solid that has a curved surface (lateral face), not flat. It is a **non-polyhedron.** Examples of curved solids are **cylinders**, **cones**, and **spheres**.

Faces, Edges, and Vertices
A **face** is the flat surface on a solid figure. **Lateral faces** are the flat surfaces that are not bases. A curved circular solid has one lateral face. The dashed lines represent edges that are on the back side of the figure.

Curved Solids

Right Circular Cylinder	Cone	Sphere
two opposite circular bases that are parallel and congruent; a curved surface	one circular base, a curved surface, a vertex that is opposite of the base	all its points are equal distance from the center point; a curved surface

Types of Cylinders
Cylinders can have bases other than circular shapes.

Examples of Other Cylinders	Examples of Other Cylinder Bases
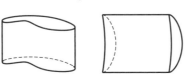	

Create Your Left-hand Notebook Page

Step 1: Cut out the title and glue it to the top of the notebook page.

Step 2: Fill in the blanks on the *Curved Solid Objects* definition piece. Cut out the piece. Apply glue to the back and attach it below the title.

Step 3: Cut out the flap pieces. Match each picture with the correct definition. Apply glue to the back of each piece and attach each pair at the bottom part of the page.

Step 4: Under the flaps of each matched pair, list some examples of objects that have the shapes of these curved solid objects.

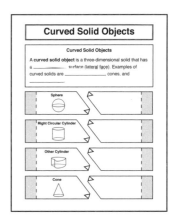

Curved Solid Objects

Curved Solid Objects

A **curved solid object** is a three-dimensional solid that has a _____ surface (lateral face). Examples of curved solids are _____, cones, and _____.

Sphere

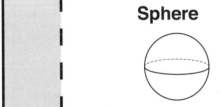

A curved solid that is a cylinder with bases other than circular shapes

Right Circular Cylinder

A curved solid with one circular base, a curved surface, and a vertex that is opposite the base

Other Cylinder

A curved solid with all points equal distance from the center point; has a curved surface

Cone

A curved solid with two opposite circular bases that are parallel and congruent; has a curved surface

Student Instructions: Platonic Solids

Read the following information. Cut out the mini-lesson and attach it to the right-hand page of your interactive notebook. Use what you have learned to create the left-hand page.

‐ ‐ ‐ ‐ ‐ ‐ ‐ ‐ ‐ ‐ ‐ ‐ ‐ ‐ ‐ ‐ ‐ ✂

Mini-Lesson

Platonic Solids

A **platonic solid** is a three-dimensional (3-D) polyhedron with flat faces. Each face is the same regular polygon.

Classifying Platonic Solids

Platonic Solids	Tetrahedron	Hexahedron (cube)
There are five platonic solids. Each figure is named after its number of faces.	four faces, which are equilateral triangles	six faces, which are squares
Octahedron	**Dodecahedron**	**Icosahedron**
eight faces, which are equilateral triangles	twelve faces, which are regular pentagons	twenty faces, which are equilateral triangles

L ‐ ‐ ‐ ‐ ‐ ‐ ‐ ‐ ‐ ‐ ‐ ‐ ‐ ‐ ‐ ‐ ‐ ‐

Create Your Left-hand Notebook Page

Step 1: Cut out the title and glue it to the top of the notebook page.

Step 2: Fill in the blanks on the *3-D Polyhedron* definition piece. Cut out the piece. Apply glue to the back and attach it below the title.

Step 3: Cut out the *Classifying Platonic Solids* flap book. Cut on the solid lines to create five flaps. Apply glue to the back of the gray center section and attach it at the bottom of the page.

Step 4: Under each flap, write the name of the platonic solid.

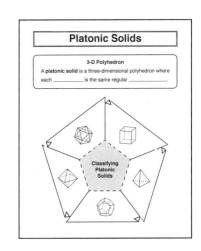

Platonic Solids

3-D Polyhedron

A **platonic solid** is a three-dimensional polyhedron where each _____ is the same regular _____.

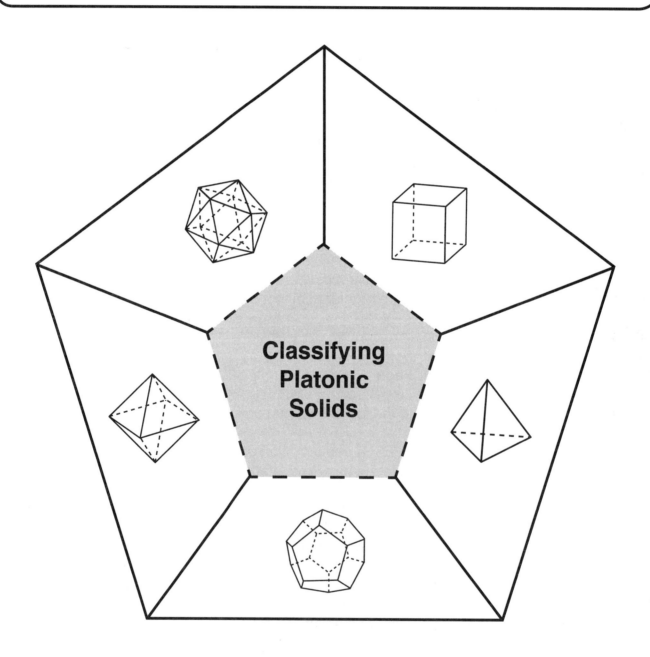

Classifying Platonic Solids

Student Instructions: Perimeter of Polygons

Read the following information. Cut out the mini-lesson and attach it to the right-hand page of your interactive notebook. Use what you have learned to create the left-hand page.

Mini-Lesson

Perimeter of Polygons

The **perimeter** (P) of a polygon is the measure of the distance around the outside of the figure. To find the perimeter, add the lengths of all sides. It can be measured in any standard distance measurement such as inches or centimeters. The answer is labeled with the measurement used in the problem.

Polygons can be classified as regular or irregular. In a **regular polygon,** where all the sides are congruent and all the interior angles are congruent, you can find the perimeter by multiplying the length of one side by the number of sides. In an **irregular polygon**, where all sides are not congruent and all angles are not congruent, add the lengths of all the sides to find the perimeter.

Finding Perimeter Using Formulas

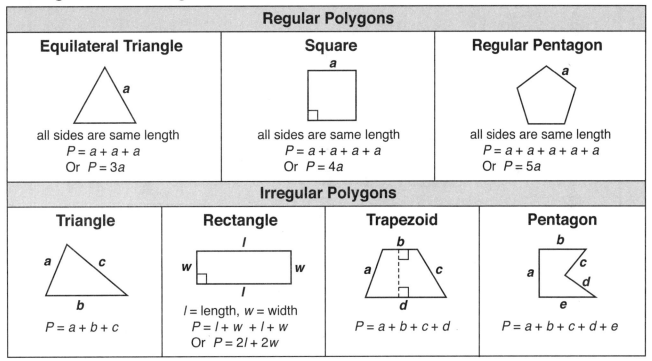

Regular Polygons		
Equilateral Triangle	**Square**	**Regular Pentagon**
all sides are same length $P = a + a + a$ Or $P = 3a$	all sides are same length $P = a + a + a + a$ Or $P = 4a$	all sides are same length $P = a + a + a + a + a$ Or $P = 5a$

Irregular Polygons			
Triangle	**Rectangle**	**Trapezoid**	**Pentagon**
$P = a + b + c$	l = length, w = width $P = l + w + l + w$ Or $P = 2l + 2w$	$P = a + b + c + d$	$P = a + b + c + d + e$

Create Your Left-hand Notebook Page

Step 1: Cut out the title and glue it to the top of the notebook page.

Step 2: Fill in the blanks on the *Perimeter* definition piece. Apply glue to the back and attach it below the title.

Step 3: Cut out the *Find the Perimeter* flap book. Cut on the solid lines to create six flaps. Apply glue to the back of the gray center section and attach it at the bottom of the page.

Step 4: Under each flap, write the formula and calculate the perimeter.

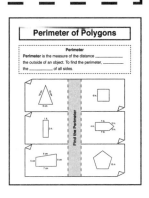

Perimeter of Polygons

Perimeter

Perimeter is the measure of the distance _____ the outside of an object. To find the perimeter, _____ the _____ of all sides.

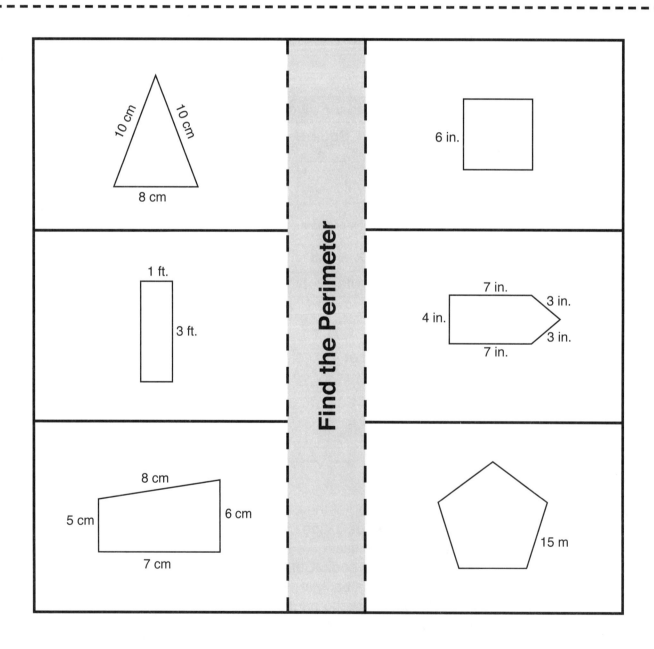

Student Instructions: Area of Triangles

Read the following information. Cut out the mini-lesson and attach it to the right-hand page of your interactive notebook. Use what you have learned to create the left-hand page.

Mini-Lesson

Area of Triangles

A **triangle** is a three-sided polygon. The **area** of a triangle is the amount of surface the figure covers. Area is measured in **square units** (sq. units) such as square inches (in²), square feet (ft²), square centimeters (cm²), or square meters (m²).

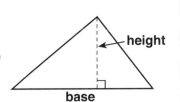

Finding Area Using a Formula
To calculate the area of a triangle, multiply ½ by the **base** of the triangle (*b*) by the **height** of the triangle (*h*). The formula for finding the area of a triangle is $A = \frac{1}{2}bh$ or $A = \frac{b \times h}{2}$.

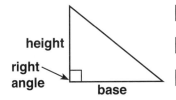

Right Triangle	Acute Triangle	Obtuse Triangle
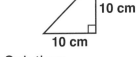		
Solution: $A = \frac{1}{2}bh$ $A = \frac{10 \times 10}{2}$ $A = \frac{100}{2}$ $A = 50$ cm²	Solution: $A = \frac{1}{2}bh$ $A = \frac{8 \times 7}{2}$ $A = \frac{56}{2}$ $A = 28$ yd.²	Solution: $A = \frac{1}{2}bh$ $A = \frac{5 \times 12}{2}$ $A = \frac{60}{2}$ $A = 30$ in.²

Create Your Left-hand Notebook Page

Step 1: Cut out the title and glue it to the top of the notebook page.

Step 2: In each box of the *Types of Triangles* puzzle piece, draw the correct triangle. Cut out the piece. Apply glue to the back and attach it below the title.

Step 3: Fill in the *Find the Area* puzzle piece. Write the formula and calculate the area of the triangle. Cut out the piece. Apply glue to the back and attach it at the bottom of the page.

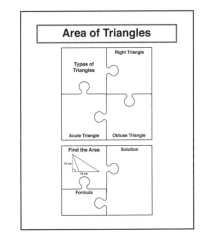

Area of Triangles

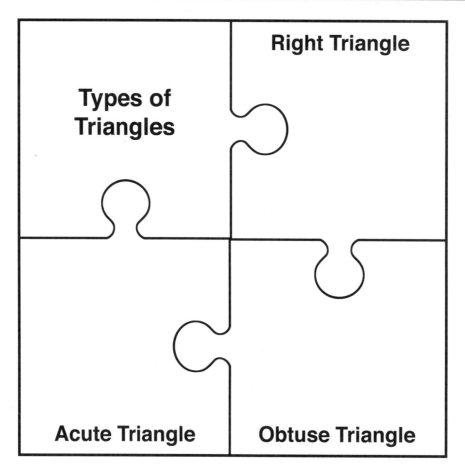

Types of Triangles

Right Triangle

Acute Triangle

Obtuse Triangle

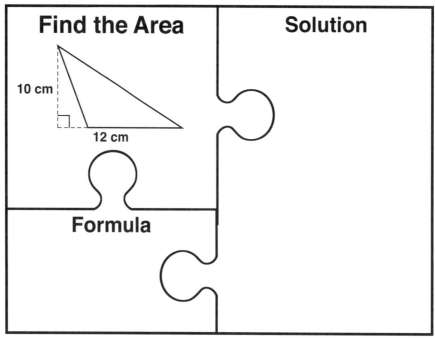

Find the Area

10 cm

12 cm

Solution

Formula

Student Instructions: Area of Quadrilaterals

Read the following information. Cut out the mini-lesson and attach it to the right-hand page of your interactive notebook. Use what you have learned to create the left-hand page.

Mini-Lesson

Area of Quadrilaterals

A **quadrilateral** is a polygon with four sides and four **vertices** or corners. The **area** of a quadrilateral is the amount of surface the figure covers. The area is measured in **square units** (sq. units) such as square inches (in^2) or square centimeters (cm^2). When finding the area of quadrilaterals, the base and height must be **perpendicular** to each other or meet at 90 degrees to form a right angle. The **base** is a side of the quadrilateral. However, depending on the quadrilateral, the height may or may not be a side.

Quadrilateral	Find Area Using a Formula
Rectangle	$Area = l \times w$ l = length, w = width The length and width are often referred to as "base" and "height" and sometimes the height is referred to as the "altitude."
Square	$Area = s \times s$ s = side The length and width are always the same number for a square; we usually call them "sides."
Parallelogram	$Area = b \times h$ b = base, h = height Sometimes the height is referred to as the "altitude."
Trapezoid	$Area = \frac{1}{2}(b_1 + b_2) \times h$ b_1 = base 1, b_2 = base 2, h = height Sometimes the height is referred to as the "altitude."

Create Your Left-hand Notebook Page

Step 1: Cut out the title and glue it to the top of the notebook page.

Step 2: Fill in the blanks on the *Quadrilaterals* piece. Cut out the piece and apply glue to the back. Attach the piece below the title.

Step 3: Fill in the formula squares on the *Finding Area of Quadrilaterals* flap book. Cut out the flap book. Cut on the bold solid lines to create four flaps. Apply glue to the back of the gray tab and attach the book at the bottom of the page.

Step 4: Under each flap, find the area of the quadrilateral.

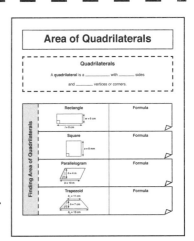

Area of Quadrilaterals

Quadrilaterals

A **quadrilateral** is a _____ with _____ sides and _____ vertices or corners.

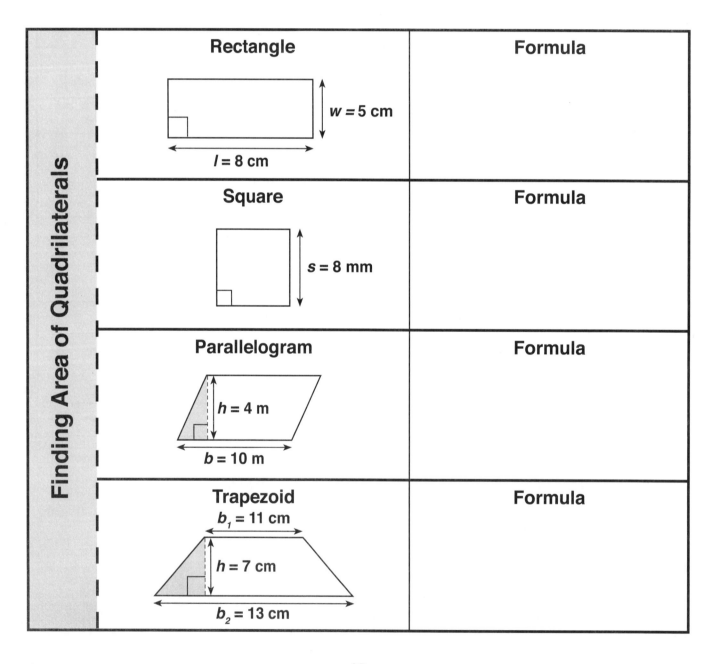

Finding Area of Quadrilaterals	Rectangle	Formula
	Square	Formula
	Parallelogram	Formula
	Trapezoid	Formula

Rectangle: *w* = 5 cm, *l* = 8 cm

Square: *s* = 8 mm

Parallelogram: *h* = 4 m, *b* = 10 m

Trapezoid: b_1 = 11 cm, *h* = 7 cm, b_2 = 13 cm

Student Instructions: Surface Area of Prisms

Read the following information. Cut out the mini-lesson and attach it to the right-hand page of your interactive notebook. Use what you have learned to create the left-hand page.

Mini-Lesson

Surface Area of Prisms

A **three-dimensional** (3-D) figure has three-dimensions: width, depth, and height. A **prism** is a three-dimensional figure with two parallel **bases** (faces) that are congruent polygons and **faces** (flat surfaces) that are parallelograms. The **surface area** (SA) of a prism is the total area of its faces. Surface area is measured in **square units** (sq. units) such as in², ft², cm², and m². To see all the faces of a prism, use a net. A **net** is the pattern made when the surface of a three-dimensional figure is laid out flat, showing each face of the figure.

Strategy for Finding Surface Area of a Prism

Step #1: Draw a net of the shape if one is not provided in the problem.

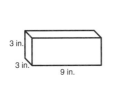

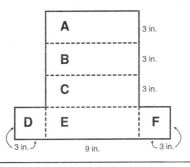

Label each face with a letter of the alphabet.

Step #2: Use a formula to calculate the area of each face. For a rectangular prism, use the formula $A = l \times w$.

A: $A = 9 \cdot 3 = 27$
B: $A = 9 \cdot 3 = 27$
C: $A = 9 \cdot 3 = 27$
D: $A = 3 \cdot 3 = 9$
E: $A = 9 \cdot 3 = 27$
F: $A = 3 \cdot 3 = 9$

Step #3: Add up the area of all the faces. State your answer in square units.
$$SA = 27 + 27 + 27 + 9 + 27 + 9$$
The surface area is 126 in².

Create Your Left-Hand Notebook Page

Step 1: Cut out the title and glue it to the top of the notebook page.

Step 2: Fill in the blank on the *Prisms* piece. Cut out the piece. Apply glue to the back and attach it below the title.

Step 3: Complete the three *Find Area* step pieces. Cut out the pieces. Apply glue to the backs and attach them at the bottom of the page.

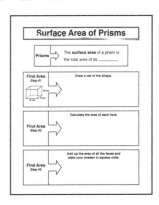

Surface Area of Prisms

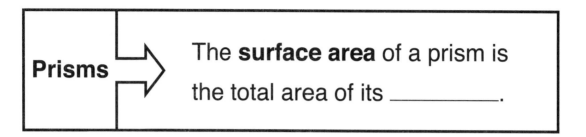

Prisms → The **surface area** of a prism is the total area of its _____.

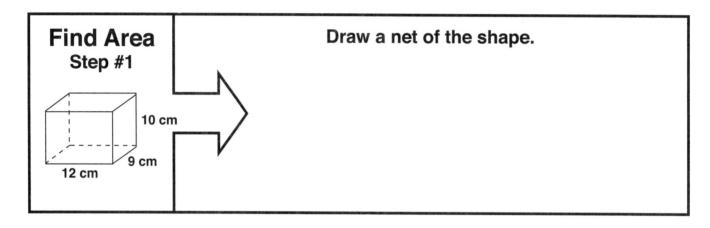

Find Area
Step #1

Draw a net of the shape.

10 cm
9 cm
12 cm

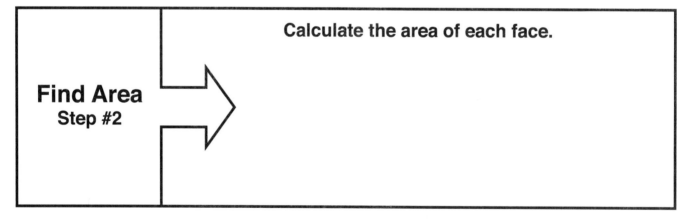

Find Area
Step #2

Calculate the area of each face.

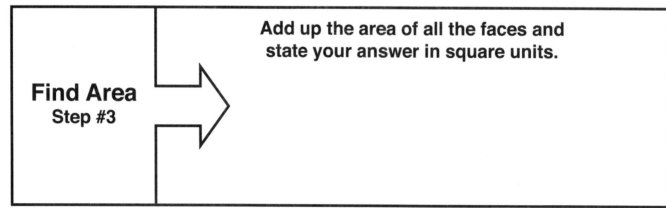

Find Area
Step #3

Add up the area of all the faces and state your answer in square units.

Student Instructions: Surface Area of Pyramids

Read the following information. Cut out the mini-lesson and attach it to the right-hand page of your interactive notebook. Use what you have learned to create the left-hand page.

Mini-Lesson

Surface Area of Pyramids

A **pyramid** is a three-dimensional figure with triangles for **lateral faces** (faces that are not bases) and one **base**. The **surface area** (SA) of a pyramid is the total area of its faces. Surface area is measured in **square units** (sq. units) such as in^2, ft^2, cm^2, and m^2.

> **Strategy for Finding Volume of a Pyramid**
>
> The surface area of any pyramid can be calculated by adding the surface area of the base (B) to the surface area of all the lateral faces.
>
> SA = area of the base + sum of the surface areas of each face

Step #1: Draw a net (a pattern showing each face of the figure). 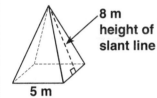 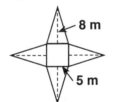	Step #2: Find the area of the base. Multiply the length of the base by the height of the base. **Area of Base** $A = l \times w$ $A = 5 \times 5$ $A = 25\ m^2$
Step #3: Find the area of one lateral face of the triangle. Multiply ½ the base of the lateral face by the height of the lateral face, where height is the slant height.	**Area of Triangle** $A = \tfrac{1}{2}bh$ or $\dfrac{b \times h}{2}$ $A = \dfrac{5 \times 8}{2}$ $A = 20\ m^2$

Step #4: Find the total surface area by adding the surface area of the base and the surface area of each lateral face. State your answer in square units.

$$SA = 25 + 20 + 20 + 20 + 20 \text{ or } SA = 25 + (4 \times 20) \quad \text{Surface area is } 105\ m^2.$$

Create Your Left-hand Notebook Page

Step 1: Cut out the title and glue it to the top of the notebook page.

Step 2: Complete each step on the *Finding Surface Area of Pyramids* piece.

Step 3: Cut out the piece, apply glue to the back, and attach it below the title.

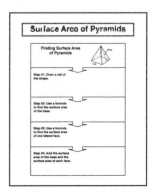

Surface Area of Pyramids

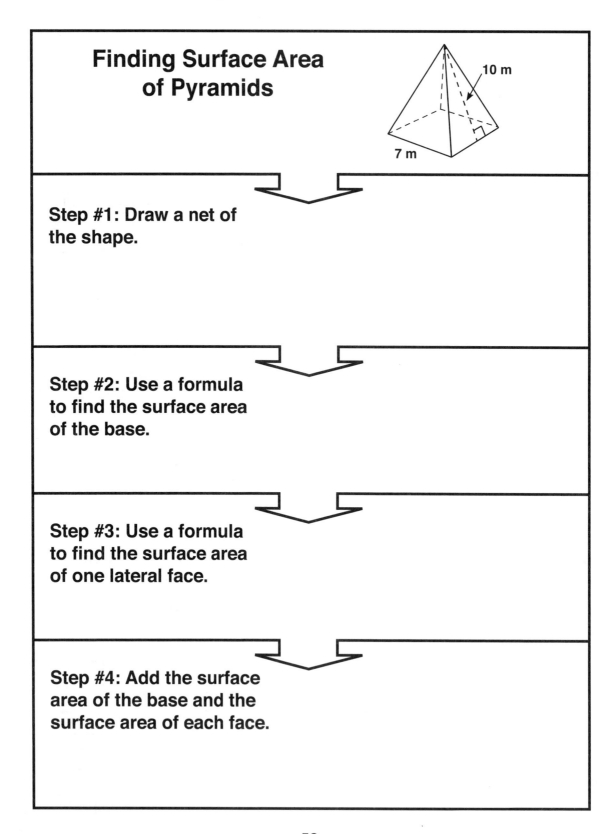

Finding Surface Area of Pyramids

10 m

7 m

Step #1: Draw a net of the shape.

Step #2: Use a formula to find the surface area of the base.

Step #3: Use a formula to find the surface area of one lateral face.

Step #4: Add the surface area of the base and the surface area of each face.

Student Instructions: Surface Area of Cones and Cylinders

Read the following information. Cut out the mini-lesson and attach it to the right-hand page of your interactive notebook. Use what you have learned to create the left-hand page.

Mini-Lesson

Surface Area of Cones and Cylinders

Cones and **cylinders** are three-dimensional (3-D) solids with a curved surface (lateral face), not flat. The **surface area** (SA) of a cone or cylinder is the total area of the faces. The area is measured in **square units** (sq. units) such as in^2, ft^2, cm^2, and m^2. To see all the faces of a cone or cylinder, use a net. A **net** is the pattern made when the surface of a three-dimensional figure is laid out flat, showing each face of the figure.

Strategies for Finding Surface Area of a Cone and Cylinder

Step #1: Draw and label a net of the shape if one is not provided in the problem.

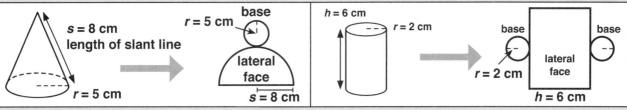

Step #2: Use a formula to calculate the total surface area of the figures. Use 3.14 for pi (π). State answers in cubic units.

The surface area of a cone equals the surface area of the circular base plus the surface area of the lateral face (outside of cone). The formula is $SA = \pi r^2 + \pi rs$. This is the same as saying the surface area of a cone equals (3.14 x radius x radius) + (3.14 x radius x slant).

$SA = \pi r^2 + \pi rs$
$SA = (3.14 \times 5 \times 5) + (3.14 \times 5 \times 8)$
$SA = 78.5 + 125.6$
$SA = 204.1 \text{ cm}^2$

The surface area of a cylinder equals two times the area of one circular base plus the area of the lateral area. The formula is $SA = 2(\pi r^2) + 2(\pi rh)$. This is the same as saying the surface area of a cylinder equals 2 x (3.14 x radius x radius) + 2 x (3.14 x radius x height).

$SA = 2(\pi r^2) + 2(\pi rh)$
$SA = 2(3.14 \times 2 \times 2) + 2(3.14 \times 2 \times 6)$
$SA = 2(12.56) + 2(37.68)$
$SA = 25.12 + 75.36$
$SA = 100.48 \text{ cm}^2$

Create Your Left-hand Notebook Page

Step 1: Cut out the title and glue it to the top of the notebook page.

Step 2: Complete the two *Surface Area* arrow pieces by drawing the net for the figure. Cut out the pieces. Apply glue to the back of the gray tabs and attach them below the title.

Step 3: Under each flap, use the correct formula to calculate the surface area of the figure.

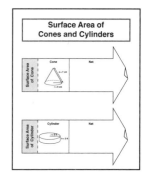

Surface Area of Cones and Cylinders

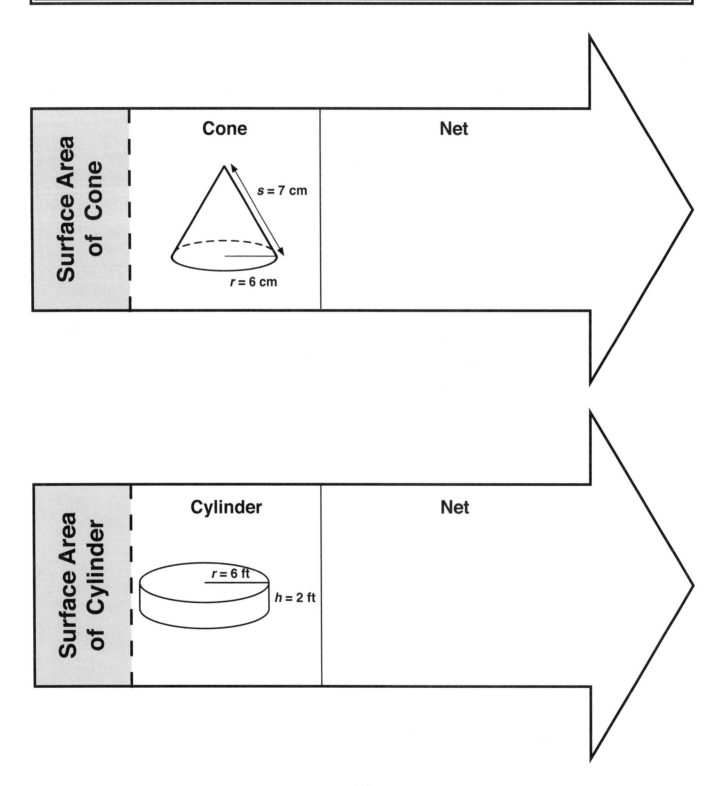

Surface Area of Cone

Cone

$s = 7$ cm

$r = 6$ cm

Net

Surface Area of Cylinder

Cylinder

$r = 6$ ft

$h = 2$ ft

Net

Student Instructions: Volume of Rectangular Prisms

Read the following information. Cut out the mini-lesson and attach it to the right-hand page of your interactive notebook. Use what you have learned to create the left-hand page.

Mini-Lesson

Volume of Rectangular Prisms

A **rectangular prism** is a three-dimensional figure with two identical bases (ends) and all flat faces (surfaces). The prism is named after the shape of its base, a rectangle. The **volume** of a rectangular prism is the amount of space inside the figure. Volume is measured in **cubic units** (cu) such as in^3, ft^3, cm^3, and m^3.

Measurements of a Rectangular Prism

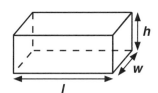

Height (h) – the part of the rectangular prism that rises up.

Width (w) – the shorter side of the flat surface, on top or bottom.

Length (l) – the longer side of the flat surface, on top or bottom.

Strategy for Finding Volume of a Rectangular Prism

To find the volume of a rectangular prism, multiply the length, width, and height of the figure. State your answer in cubic units. The formula is $V = l$ x w x h.

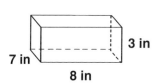

Step #1: Write down the formula for finding the volume of a rectangular prism.

$V = l$ x w x h

Step #2: Find the length, width, and height of the rectangular prism.

$V = 8$ x 7 x 3

Step #3: Multiply the length, the width, and the height of the rectangular prism. You can multiply them in any order. State your answer in cubic units.

$V = 168$ in^3

Create Your Left-hand Notebook Page

Step 1: Cut out the title and glue it to the top of the notebook page.

Step 2: Fill in the blanks on the *Rectangular Prism* piece. Cut out the three word pieces. Apply glue to the backs and place them in the correct boxes on the diagram. Cut out the piece. Apply glue to the back and attach it below the title.

Step 4: Complete the two blank *Formula* and *Volume* arrow pieces. Cut out all three pieces. Apply glue to the backs and glue them at the bottom of the page.

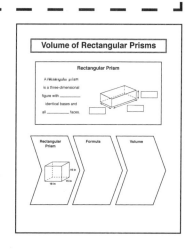

Volume of Rectangular Prisms

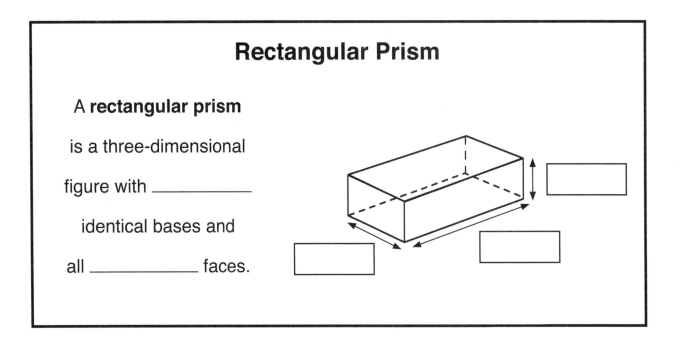

Rectangular Prism

A **rectangular prism** is a three-dimensional figure with _____ identical bases and all _____ faces.

| height | width | length |

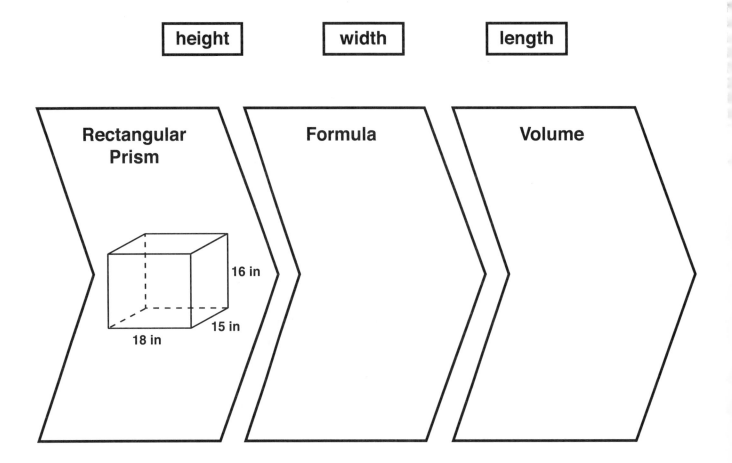

Student Instructions: Volume of Triangular Prisms

Read the following information. Cut out the mini-lesson and attach it to the right-hand page of your interactive notebook. Use what you have learned to create the left-hand page.

✂

Mini-Lesson

Volume of Triangular Prisms

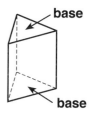

base

base

A **triangular prism** is a three-dimensional figure. It is a polyhedron with three rectangular faces and two parallel triangular bases. The **volume** of a triangular prism is the amount of space inside the figure. Volume is measured in **cubic units** (cu) such as in^3, ft^3, cm^3, and m^3.

Strategy for Finding Volume of a Triangular Prism
Calculating the volume of a triangular prism is a two-step process. First, find the area of one of the triangular bases. Second, multiply the area of the base (B) by the height (h), which is the length (long side) of the prism. The formula is $V = Bh$. State your answer in cubic units.

Step #1: Find the area of one triangular base. Multiple ½ by the base of the triangle by the height of the triangle.

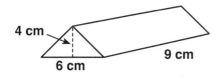

4 cm

6 cm

9 cm

$$A = \tfrac{1}{2}bh \text{ or } \frac{bh}{2}$$

$$A = \frac{6 \times 4}{2}$$

$$A = 12 \text{ cm}^2$$

Step #2: Multiply the area of the triangular base (12 cm^2) by the height (length) of the rectangular prism.

$$V = Bh$$
$$V = 12 \text{ (area of the triangular base) x 9 (height of the rectangular prism)}$$
$$V = 108 \text{ cm}^3$$

Create Your Left-hand Notebook Page

Step 1: Cut out the title and glue it to the top of the notebook page.

Step 2: Cut out the three *Question* flap pieces. Apply glue to the back of the gray tabs and attach them below the title. Under each flap, answer the question.

Step 3: Fill in the boxes on the *Volume of Triangular Prisms* chart. Cut out the chart. Apply glue to the back and attach it below the title.

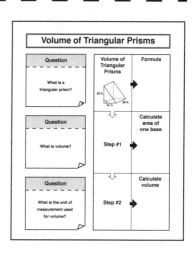

Volume of Triangular Prisms

Question
What is a triangular prism?

Question
What is volume?

Question
What is the unit of measurement used for volume?

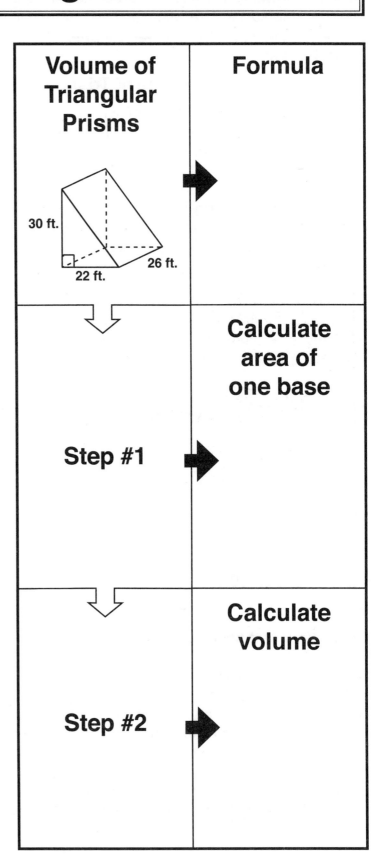

Student Instructions: Volume of Cones and Cylinders

Read the following information. Cut out the mini-lesson and attach it to the right-hand page of your interactive notebook. Use what you have learned to create the left-hand page.

Mini-Lesson

Volume of Cones and Cylinders

Cones and **cylinders** are three-dimensional figures. **Volume** is the measure of the amount of space inside of a figure. Volume is measured in **cubic units** (cu) such as in^3, ft^3, cm^3, and m^3.

Strategy for Finding Volume of a Cone

To find the volume of a cone, calculate the area of the base and then multiply $\frac{1}{3}$ by the area of the base by the height. The formula is: $V = \frac{1}{3}Bh$ or $\frac{1}{3}\pi r^2 \times h$. This is the same as (3.14 x radius x radius x height) ÷ 3. Use 3.14 for pi (π). State volume in cubic units.

	Identify Radius of Base	Find Area of Base	Identify Height	Find Volume
5 ft (height) / 2 ft (radius)	2 ft	$A = \pi r^2$ $A = 3.14 \times 2^2$ $A = 3.14 \times 4$ $A = 12.56 \ ft^2$	5 ft	$V = \frac{1}{3}Bh$ $V = \frac{12.56 \times 5}{3}$ $V = \frac{62.8}{3}$ $V = 20.93 \ ft^3$

Strategy for Finding Volume of a Cylinder

To find the volume of a cylinder, calculate the area of the base and then multiply the area of the base by the height of the cylinder. The formula is: $V = Bh$ or $V = \pi r^2 \times h$. This is the same as 3.14 x radius x radius x height. Use 3.14 for pi (π). State volume in cubic units.

	Identify Radius of Base	Find Area of Base	Identify Height	Find Volume
3 m / 6 m	3 m	$A = \pi r^2$ $A = 3.14 \times 3^2$ $A = 3.14 \times 9$ $A = 28.26 \ m^2$	6 m	$V = Bh$ $V = 28.26 \times 6$ $V = 169.56 \ m^3$

Create Your Left-hand Notebook Page

Step 1: Cut out the title and glue it to the top of the notebook page.

Step 2: Complete the *Cone* and *Cylinder* charts. Cut out the charts. Apply glue to the backs and attach them below the title.

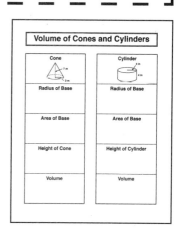

Volume of Cones and Cylinders

Cone	Cylinder
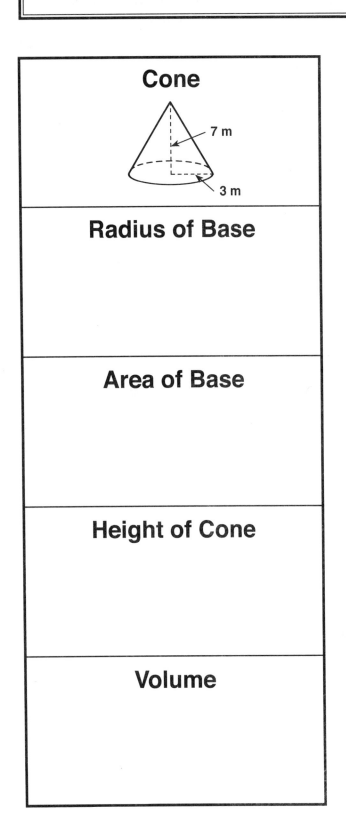	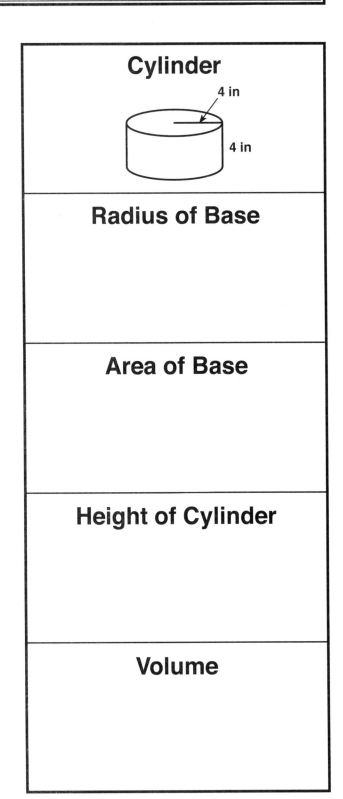
Radius of Base	**Radius of Base**
Area of Base	**Area of Base**
Height of Cone	**Height of Cylinder**
Volume	**Volume**

Answer Keys

Answers are limited to those not presented as part of the mini-lessons on each "Student Instructions" page.

Measuring Angles (p. 10)
$m\angle DEC = 40°$ $m\angle DEG = 130°$
$m\angle GEF = 50°$

Congruent or Similar? (p. 22)
Congruent:

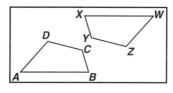

Similar:

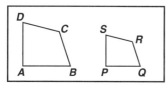

Radius and Diameter (p. 28)
Diameter: 5.8 cm
Radius: 7.5 mm

Circumference of a Circle (p. 30)
Circumference using diameter: 23.9 cm
Circumference using radius: 100.5 m

Area of a Circle (p. 32)
452.16 cm²   379.94 m²

Three-Dimensional Figures (p. 34)
1. 8 vertices, 12 edges, 6 faces
2. 0 vertices, 0 edges, 3 faces
3. 10 vertices, 15 edges, 7 faces

Curved Solid Objects (p. 40)
Examples may vary, but could include:
Sphere: ball, globe
Right Circular Cylinder: vegetable can
Other Cylinder: oval shampoo bottle
Cone: traffic cone, snow cone holder

Perimeter of Polygons (p. 44)
Left Side: 28 cm
            8 ft
            26 cm
Right Side: 24 in
            24 in
            75 m

Area of Triangles (p. 46)
Solution: 60 cm²

Area of Quadrilaterals (p. 48)
Rectangle: 40 cm²
Square: 64 mm²
Parallelogram: 40 m²
Trapezoid: 84 cm²

Surface Area of Prisms (p. 50)
Nets and the labeling of each face may vary, but the surface area should come out the same no matter how the faces are labeled.
Step #1:

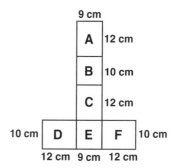

Step #2:
A: $A = 9 \times 12 = 108$ cm²
B: $A = 9 \times 10 = 90$ cm²
C: $A = 9 \times 12 = 108$ cm²
D: $A = 12 \times 10 = 120$ cm²
E: $A = 9 \times 10 = 90$ cm²
F: $A = 12 \times 10 = 120$ cm²

Step #3:
$SA = 108 + 90 + 108 + 120 + 90 + 120$
$SA = 636$ cm²

Answer Keys (cont.)

Surface Area of Pyramids (p. 52)

Step #1:

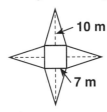

Step #2: $A = l \times w$, $A = 7 \times 7$, $A = 49$ m^2
Step #3: $A = \frac{1}{2}bh$, $A = \frac{1}{2}(7 \times 10)$, $A = 35$ m^2
Step #4: $SA = 49 + 35 + 35 + 35 + 35 = 189$ m^2
 or $SA = 49 + (4 \times 35) = 189$ m^2

Surface Area of Cones and Cylinders (p. 54)

Cone Net:

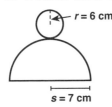

Formula and Solution:
 $SA = \pi r^2 = \pi r s$
 $SA = (3.14 \times 6 \times 6) + (3.14 \times 6 \times 7)$
 $SA = 113.04 + 131.88$
 $SA = 244.92$ cm^2

Cylinder Net:

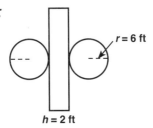

Formula and Solution:
 $SA = 2(\pi r^2) + 2(\pi r h)$
 $SA = 2(3.14 \times 6 \times 6) + 2(3.14 \times 6 \times 2)$
 $SA = 226.08 + 75.36$
 $SA = 301.44$ ft^2

Volume of Rectangular Prisms (p. 56)

Formula: $V = l \times w \times h$
Volume: $V = 18 \times 15 \times 16$
 $V = 4{,}320$ in^3

Volume of Triangular Prisms (p. 58)

Formula: $V = Bh$
Step #1:
 Area of Base: $A = \frac{1}{2}bh$
 $A = \frac{1}{2}(22 \times 30)$
 $A = \frac{660}{2}$
 $A = 330$ ft^2
Step #2:
 Volume: $V = 330 \times 26$
 $V = 8{,}580$ ft^3

Volume of Cones and Cylinders (p. 60)

Cone:
 Radius: 3 m
 Area of Base: $A = \pi r^2$
 $A = 3.14 \times 3^2$
 $A = 3.14 \times 9$
 $A = 28.26$ m^2
 Height: 7 m
 Volume: $V = \frac{1}{3}Bh$
 $V = \frac{1}{3}(28.26 \times 7)$
 $V = \frac{197.82}{3}$
 $V = 65.94$ m^3

Cylinder:
 Radius: 4 in
 Area of Base: $A = \pi r^2$
 $A = 3.14 \times 4^2$
 $A = 3.14 \times 16$
 $A = 50.24$ in^2
 Height: 4 in
 Volume: $V = Bh$
 $V = 50.24 \times 4$
 $V = 200.96$ in^3